UNLOCK
THE
POWER
OF
FAMILY

UNLOCK
THE
POWER
OF
FAMILY

Daniel A. Brown, Ph.D.

WORD PUBLISHING
Nelson Word Ltd
Milton Keynes, England

ALPHA & OMEGA DISTRIBUTORS
Queensland, Australia

STRUIK CHRISTIAN BOOKS (PTY) LTD
Cape Town, South Africa

JOINT DISTRIBUTORS SINGAPORE—
ALBY COMMERCIAL ENTERPRISES PTE LTD
and
CAMPUS CRUSADE, ASIA LTD

PHILIPPINE CAMPUS CRUSADE FOR CHRIST
Quezon City, Philippines

CHRISTIAN MARKETING NEW ZEALAND LTD
Havelock North, New Zealand

JENSCO LTD
Hong Kong

SALVATION BOOK CENTRE
Malaysia

UNLOCK THE POWER OF THE FAMILY

Copyright ©1994 by Daniel A. Brown.

First published in the USA by Sparrow Press, Nashville, Tennessee.

First UK edition by Nelson Word Ltd., Milton Keynes, 1995.

ISBN 1-86024-025-9

Reproduced, printed and bound in Great Britain for Nelson Word Ltd. by Cox and Wyman Ltd., Reading

95 96 97 98 / 10 9 8 7 6 5 4 3 2 1

To Pamela—
the bride I took to be, for the rest of our lives.

Contents

Acknowledgements

When a pastor undertakes a project beyond the scope of normal church duties, those ministry responsibilities must be attended to by others. Without my pastoral team—Steve and Kathy Blackwell, Gary and Bonny Craig, Neil and Terry Richarde, Steve and Donna Shober, and Bob and Cynthia War—this book would not have been written.

The same bolds true for the entire staff of The Coastlands, but especially for my two able and willing assistants— Merrilee Tunink and Joyce McCann.

To them all, and to my family at The Coastlands, I extend my deepest thanks.

Foreword

For just a moment, surrender caution, open both arms and extend an embrace, if you will. I want to introduce you to two creative entities: this book, and its author.

You will discover here a creativity greater than mere human ingenuity or cleverness. As you'll see, both *Unlock the Power of Family* and author Daniel Brown are creative expressions of God's Holy Spirit at a time when 'new creation' is desperately needed. Let me explain.

The opening words of the Bible reveal a two-edged truth about God's mighty creation of our world: His light shone into the darkness and brought earth, life and all their splendours into being. And, He created in a context—chaos—that made the 'new creation' all the more lovely and necessary. The chaotic state of that ancient setting reminds us of the awesome power of God's creative Word to transform. That Word brings light and establishes order.

The miracle of creation offers reason for hope in any life, home or circumstance where chaos dominates. Since there is no arena of life more jumbled by chaos than the family, the need for the 'new creativity' found in this book is obvious.

You may sense my delight in introducing *Unlock the Power of Family* and my friend Daniel Brown. I could introduce Daniel on the basis of our nearly twenty years of acquaintance, which reach back to his college days. God bonded us as friends while I served him as his pastor. But I would rather introduce him as a peer in ministry, for in the intervening years, I have seen the Holy Spirit profoundly at work in Daniel's marriage, his family, his ministry and his life. I want you to know Daniel in the context of his increasingly fruitful family life, as well as his pastoral, missionary and church-planting enterprises. I could elaborate at length on any of those facets of ministry. But instead let me select a single adjective to describe him—bright: Daniel Brown is a bright young voice, a *bright* and godly leader and a *bright* and gifted writer.

Like me, you might not be charmed by the concept of 'bright young talent'. The term can be used to describe arrogant, swaggering intellects, or self-centred, carnally indulgent 'stars'. Rather than identifying the promise of a strong future leader, *bright* can engender suspicion and dubiousness among the wise. So let me qualify *bright*.

The Holy Spirit brings a divine fire and light to people who walk in the ways of God, who humble themselves as He teaches and corrects them, who listen as He guides and directs them and who honour those who have walked the way of faith before them. As that person submits to the refining of God's divine fire and yields to the purifying of the Spirit's light, a holy 'brightness' evolves.

I have watched and walked with Daniel through the years, and now I am happy to introduce to you a trustworthy teacher, a proven shepherd and a loving husband and father. In all these quarters of his life, I've watched this brightness cultivated by God's grace. It's a brightness not simply of genius but genuineness. I think you'll see that genuineness in *Unlock the Power of Family*.

We need divine light today, the kind of light that brings order out of chaos. I believe you'll welcome the bright hope these pages offer. As you read, reach to embrace a new concept of family. That new concept is *covenant*—the power of family as conceived by God.

In this book, you will find healing for dysfunction, understanding for brokenness, freedom from ruinous bonds—in short, *hope!* The hope offered is real and practical—guidance from an experienced pastor who has developed one of Northern California's strongest growing congregations, who is a husband of twenty years of successful marriage and the father of four good children.

As you open your arms to this 'brightness', you'll find more than a man and a book. You'll find yourself making contact with the Light of the World—Jesus—who brings new creation to hearts and homes where darkness has prevailed until now.

To Him be all glory,
Jack W. Hayford

The Church On The Way
Van Nuys, California
Spring 1994

Preface

Few of us deny the power of family to adversely impact our sense of identity and the ways we view life. Unpleasant family life hurts for the rest of our lives. No matter how determined we are to 'move away from home' when we grow up, we can't quite shake off what home was to us. Despite our best efforts, things said and done in the family we grew up in continually play on our minds.

As more attention is focused on the breakdown of normal, life-giving relationships between parent and child or husband and wife, a new vocabulary is developing to describe what is going wrong with the family. Philosophers tell us that we cannot think about something until we have language to name and identify it. Some even argue that the essential difference between emotions and thoughts is language. Thus, having a terminology to describe the nebulous aches or the profound stirrings of joy we feel about our childhood and family gives hope for us to avoid what went wrong—or to recreate for our own families what went right—when we were young.

Meaningful talk about family—the kind of talk that will really help you love your spouse and raise your children—is difficult. Scholars and psychologists have developed terms such as *dysfunctional family*, *co-dependency*, *family systems* and *addictions* to identify the dynamics of family. As with any new field of study, the vocabulary evolves as understanding increases. Christians sometimes have a knee-jerk reaction to new terms (especially when they don't sound theological), and we become suspicious of what is said because the language is unfamiliar—and judged to be *secular*.

Rather than argue over vocabulary, we need to offer

adequate answers—spiritual answers expressed in contemporary language—to a world that asks why families are falling apart.

On the other hand, we cannot afford to lose our prophetic voice to the world. If we wait for secular researchers and philosophers to identify and define the dynamics of family, we will find ourselves simply Christianising their language and their theories. Instead of following their lead, we ought to cry out in the wilderness of ruined families, telling people the way God meant things to be.

Estimates of dysfunctional families in America range from eighty per cent to ninety-five per cent of the total population, an incredible admission by a society that has rejected God's plan for life in favour of self-improvement. The catch has always been that even if humanity had the capacity to repair family, it wouldn't know what God had in mind for family from the beginning of time.

What does *family* mean? Is it a montage of lifelong experiences, a closed circle of domestic relationships, a description of a small social system (mum and dad and 2.4 children)? Or is its meaning something else, something hidden from our secularised view of growing up? What did God have in mind when He said it was not good for Adam to live alone? If we do not understand what *family* really is, we will be blind to its power—at least, its power for great good.

Almost everyone acknowledges that something is wrong in family, but we can offer good news. This book seeks to answer two questions:

- What explains the power of family to mess people up so profoundly?
- Can that power be harnessed for good?

You flood the Lord's altar with tears.
You weep and wail because he no
longer pays attention to your offerings. . .
You ask, 'Why?' It is because the
Lord is acting as the witness between
you and the wife of your youth,
because you have broken faith with
her, though she is your partner,
the wife of your marriage covenant.

Malachi 2:13–14

1

Something Is Broken

At forty-three, Duane knows what it is like to be both victim and victimiser in a family. Though his father had been kind and passive, Duane was often another sort of dad to his own children. Usually, Duane was gentle and affectionate, often communicating his love for his children. Then, without warning, he would rage against his children—assaulting them with hateful shouts, angry words and fierce restrictions. The bouts often ended with smouldering eyes, flashes of half-begun sentences, and with Duane stomping out of the room. Although he did not physically abuse them, the damage he did to his children was just as severe, leaving them confused, insecure and demoralised.

After he calmed down, Duane felt terrible about the outbursts. He confessed his anger to his wife and children, and asked them—repeatedly—to forgive him. He did his best to control his temper. Yet the cycle continued.

When he thought about why he treated the family he loved in such a horrible way, Duane realised that he was repeating a pattern of rage his mother started years before when he was young. She too had been unpredictable. The memories of her angry words and emotional threats still stung him. And that made his behaviour towards his own children even more devastating. As a child, Duane vowed never to be like his mother, yet now he felt hopeless to change. Coming from the agony of a broken family, he now watched himself breaking up his own family.

What compelled Duane to repeat with his children the mistakes his mother made with him? Was it as simple as imitative behaviour? What power does family have over our lives to destine us to live as our parents lived? And if family can so easily work *against* us, is there any way to make it work *for* us?

We keep struggling to recover from the traumas we suffered as children; we can't bear to see those same traumas in the lives of our own children. But what we feared and hated, we have become. Somehow, we missed the path that led to the kind of family we promised ourselves we would have when we were in charge. Instead, we have a response that can be explosive, like Duane's, or quietly desperate, like Cindy's.

Cindy

Though she struggled to make her family work, Cindy felt helpless to do so. Something tore at her about what family should be. But she was stuck and exhausted—unable to find the energy to figure things out.

Cindy, who had an effervescent personality, taught fine arts at a local high school. At thirty-two she appeared to have everything under control. Her house and her life were tightly arranged and immaculate. Her husband, a college graduate, had a fast-track job with a software development firm. Her two children, aged five and eight, attended the best private schools. And, her principal told her that she should expect a promotion to the head of her department.

All was well, until the day the doctor confirmed her suspicions—she was pregnant. The emotions that surged through her caught her off guard.

Several weeks later as she talked out her feelings with a

friend, Cindy tearfully admitted she didn't want any more children. The two children she had already were more confusing and disappointing to her than she ever expected. She had resigned herself to not being a great parent. She thought of her mother, remembering the alcohol abuse and the uncertainty, and Cindy concluded that some people weren't cut out to be good parents. She must be one of those people—like her mother. Maybe it was inherited, like diabetes. Whatever it was, Cindy could find no enthusiasm for having another child.

Cindy had been looking forward to less responsibility for the two children she already had, and the opportunity to get on with her career. The thought of having another child threw her into a panic. She didn't think she could handle the stress another child would place on her marriage, or the fresh opportunities it would create for sibling rivalry and arguments.

She oscillated between guilt at thinking that way, and dread of the problems another child would bring. But mostly, Cindy feared that her ambivalence toward her children mirrored the neglect and the lack of caring she felt from her own mother. How could she do to her kids what her alcoholic mum had done to her? Wasn't it enough that she had never taken a drink herself? Why was family such drudgery for Cindy? She had all the outward ingredients of a happy home, but happiness eluded her.

Traumas from our childhood can manifest themselves in other ways than in our relationships with our children. All of us—whether we have children or not—bear the psycho-emotional imprint of our upbringing. And the patterns pressed into our souls by what we experienced in family can affect our interpersonal relationships. Such was the case with Gretchen.

Gretchen

On the surface, nothing about this witty, artistic woman of twenty-four remotely suggested brokenness. In fact, when she first began attending our church, her sophistication and *Vogue*-cover beauty caused *others* to feel inadequate. Gretchen was gorgeous, poised and strikingly self-assured.

A successful designer, she had (or could have) anything she wanted—except the ability to resist men's sexual advances. She simply couldn't say no. Men, invariably taken with her beauty, pressed at the edges of her physical and emotional resolve until—fairly quickly—they gained entrance to fulfil their passion.

It wasn't that Gretchen enjoyed those kinds of intimacies. Or that she found power and prestige in seduction and sex. In the recovery language of today, she probably would explain her promiscuity as 'sexual addiction'—something she loathed but found herself involved in anyway.

When Gretchen encountered the love of Jesus, she not only realised that what she was doing violated the way of life He wanted for her, but she gained new strength to resist temptation—primarily by choosing not to date at all. About eight months later, though, she fell into her familiar pattern and had sex with a man she hardly knew.

The next day she came to see me—to confess and to ask for help. Seeing the look of remorse in her eyes, I felt no need to tell her what she already knew—that she had done wrong. More than anything else, she was confused. She wanted to understand why she had stepped so easily across the boundary of truth and given herself to this man.

What was broken in her?

Without realising it, Gretchen answered that herself. 'I just wanted to be held, to be touched and caressed,' she said. 'I wanted to lie there safe in his arms. After he held me for a while, I figured I owed him. So I let him have what he wanted from me.'

Like many others, Gretchen grew up in a broken home. Her daddy wasn't around to play with her ponytail, to give her piggy-back rides, or to bring her her first bunch of roses. Gretchen's unfulfilled need to be close to her dad, because her family was broken by divorce, became an over-powering longing later in her life to be intimate with any man.

Gretchen's confusion and dismay over her own behaviour left her with self-accusation: *Why do I keep doing this?* Because she couldn't find a satisfactory answer, she concluded there was something wrong with her—something dark and loathsome.

Gretchen voiced the questions so many of us silently ask ourselves, *Why can't I have the kind of relationships that would make me happy and fulfilled, and that would bring that same happiness and fulfilment to others? Why are good, solid, growing relationships so hard to find?* Our family background often counteracts the good we try to do as we build our new families with our spouses and children. Why?

Each of these examples portrays a family broken in some way. At one time, a *broken family* simply described the physical aftermath of a divorce—Mum or Dad no longer living with the children with some psycho-emotional damage to them. Nowadays, discussion on divorce has increasingly moved *away from* the harm it causes, and *towards* the remarkable adjustments *children* can make. Brokenness has become so common that we have had to stop lamenting it, and find ways to live with it.

A family can be broken in many ways—divorce merely publicly acknowledges that breakage. That is why the term *broken* has been replaced by *dysfunctional*—meaning *not working as it was meant to work.* In fact, whether or not parents separate, the dynamic of family relationships—the codes of silence, the rules of behaviour, promises and *psyches* violated—can create major traumas.

Josslyn

Josslyn's parents weren't divorced, but Josslyn was broken, nonetheless. The oldest of three girls, she was subjected to her father's sexual violations for years, and as with most traumatised children, she learned how to survive and pretend.

Josslyn felt degraded and worthless. She felt there was no point to her life—that is, until her father began to go after her younger sisters. Then she had a purpose. For the next four years, whenever she saw her father's lustful stupor, the distant glaze in his eyes that meant he wanted one of the girls, Josslyn played the part of jealous seducer, and offered her body to protect her sisters.

Something is terribly broken when a girl is forced to have sex with her father, and when, as Josslyn did some years later, that daughter attempts to kill the man she calls Father.

Broken Families

As more people talk about what happened when they were children, we see two important truths emerging:
1) the distortions in family are more perverse than we imagined, and 2) they are more pervasive. If any doubt remains, watch the evening news. It is filled with stories of family violence and abuse. My pastoral counselling brings me into regular contact with people like Duane, Cindy and Gretchen—and with even more horrific casualties of broken families, like Josslyn.

What has happened to family? Broken, dysfunctional families seem to be the order of the day. Nearly everyone has been affected either directly or indirectly by the breakdown. Instead of healthy relationships between husband and wife, parents and children, we see widespread patterns of abuse (both verbal and physical), addiction (to substances and to emotions), and alienation (from oneself and from others). Having so few models of functional families and so little teaching about what makes family work well, we are left to copy the distortions in the families from which we came, or to create our own experimental family concepts.

Despite all the time-saving and space-saving conveniences of modern technology, and the latest theories on how to live the good life, nothing is more elusive for us than a healthy family. We want it, but we aren't sure exactly what it is. We can imagine our dream family, but how to get in it or how to create it for our children seems beyond our grasp.

So rather than asking, 'What part of family was broken in Duane's case?' 'Why did Cindy's efforts to have a good family fail?' or 'What drove Gretchen to misuse her sexuality?', we need to ask, 'What is this thing called family?' 'What makes it so powerful? And can we use that power to repair and build our relationships, rather than break them?'

Most recovery theories about the family do not consider how family is supposed to work. We know it is broken, but don't know why. Unless we know what family is, we won't know how it should work.

The Broken Car

At Christmas a few years ago, my son Collin—then ten

years old—got a remote-control car. He loved it. It lasted a day and a half.

'Dad, my car is broken.'

'How did it get broken?'

'I dunno.'

'Well, what happened?'

'I dunno. It just stopped working.'

With a knowing look, I examined the outside of the car. I pushed a few of the buttons on the remote control, looked at the car again, shrugged my shoulders and agreed, 'It's broken.'

I had neither helped the car nor my son. If I knew more about electronics, I would have known to look for the disconnected wire inside the remote control. A few days later, a friend of the family who knows about such things found the wire and fixed it—lucky for Collin, the car and me.

Many of the experts on family today respond the way I did to Collin's car. They render verdicts that the family is, indeed, broken. But that is all they can do. Like I did, they focus only on the car, and forget the remote control.

People trained in the behavioural sciences usually look at external characteristics and traits of families. Looking for natural explanations, they rarely consider anything beyond the natural, the intangibles that are a part of the supernatural. At the root of their examination is a philosophy called *empiricism*—the belief that everything can be understood in the light of and related to the physical world. They evaluate a supernatural entity like family in terms of what they can see, hear, feel, smell or taste.

They express the dynamics of family in measurable terms alone. Researchers even use clinical terminology to describe emotions. Approaching the family as though it were merely a set of social or behavioural mores, they fail to recognise that it is, at its root, a spiritual entity.

Social and behavioural scientists study people and the *natural* forces that affect them. Unfortunately, they lack the tools to see inside the heart and soul of the family—the remote control that drives the car.

Identifying Other Forces

The empirical approach's weaknesses are many. For instance, while researchers can identify a disordered relationship between a father and daughter like Josslyn, they are unable to point out the disorders in that father's relationship with God. Likewise, they dismiss foolishness and rebellion in a child as merely self-expression.

But as there are laws that govern the physical universe, so there are laws of the spiritual side of reality. For instance, we know that laws of thermodynamics order the way the physical world works. But there is also a divinely appointed order to the non-material world: *judge not lest you be judged; and what you sow you will reap.*

Interesting and helpful though psychology may be, its explanations are limited to only half of the story. What we need is a model that explains family from a spiritual perspective.

Even the most well-meaning of us can mistakenly approach family problems on the basis of *observation* rather than *intention*. For instance, if you went to a pastor for marriage counselling, you would probably be asked, *Are you reading your Bible? Are you praying together? Are you attending church together? Is your husband sensitive to your needs? Does your wife respect you?* These things are all great, but like the empiricist, they only examine the external landscape.

We pastors, like our secular counterparts, often focus on external solutions to treat internal problems. We apply plasters to deep wounds. Inadequate to treat the heart of the matter, we satisfy ourselves with labelling the external symptoms and superficially treating them.

Why is this? Because it is easier to observe and explain dysfunction than to fix it. What is wrong is easier to spot than what is right. Intuitively we sense that things are wrong with family today, but we struggle to grasp what a good family ought to be, and how it ought to work.

Anyone could have developed theories about *why* Collin's car didn't work. Since I had only a vague notion of how it was supposed to run, I would have been satisfied with almost any authoritative sounding explanation—at least until that 'expert' was unable to fix the car.

In the same way, we must be careful not to accept a theory about family whose only merit is that it admits the family is broken! Putting our finger on what is wrong may involve more than looking on the surface. If the problem is the remote-control, no amount of tinkering with the car will make any difference. Without a whole notion of family, ideas about how to fix it are meaningless.

By the way, repairing a broken family is not as easy as reparing a remote-control car. Families are not toys. But this analogy helps us understand the limitations of most experts' advice on the family.

The Power Makes the Difference

Actually, Collin received several cars that Christmas. He enjoyed playing with all of them. I know that because I found them left in almost every room in the house. But his remote-control car was his favourite.

Without the power of the transmitter to make it go,

the car would look the same, but it wouldn't work the same. It would be just another car. Families can be like that. They may look like families, but they don't have the power to be family the way God planned.

So what makes family?

We recognise that family consists of love, commitment and nurture. Family cannot be fully or satisfactorily explained as the physical and emotional joining of people. Family has other consequences, other purposes in our lives.

What power does family have? What does it all mean to those of us who want to raise our children well, or who want to recover from our upbringing?

We usually think about family in two ways—in terms of situation or function. In situational terms, a great family is a model gleaned from movies and magazines, where everything is wonderful all the time. The children never cry, the rubbish always gets taken out, problems are minor or humorous, and are easily resolved (between commercials) in half-hour episodes. The situational family is explained in physical terms—the look of the house, the age of the children, the dialogue and placement of the characters.

The functional family, idealised in our minds, is seen more in terms of what it does for us—it makes us happy, it fulfils our needs. If dinner is on time, if he listens when she talks, if she responds when he initiates intimacies, if the children pick up after themselves, if they get picked up after school for the dentist appointment—then the family is working.

As essential as those particulars may be, they do not capture the essence of family the way God meant it to be. Those sorts of externals cannot explain the tremendous impact our upbringing has on our psyche. A definition of real family ought to help us understand the effect we can have on our children and the effect our parents had on us.

When God created family, He had something definite in mind, something that answers how family systems and relationships ought to function. Not surprisingly, what we long for in family is exactly what God made family to give us.

We do not have the authority to define family on our own terms. *Love* as understood by a fourteen-year-old girl and boy is inadequate to carry and support their lives and relationship throughout adulthood. Similarly, our ideas about family fall far short of understanding all of its intended dynamics. Being members of a family grouping does not mean that we are in *real family*—family the way God created it.

Family is more than a living arrangement between people. It is more than a system of interpersonal relationships, or a common culture of a small circle of people. *Family is a force that God introduced into the world to do good to people all the days of their lives.* True family has a power that most people only dream of.

At this point, it is fair to ask what God's intention was for family. What did He have in mind when He said it was not good for people to be alone? Rather than merely observing modern families as they are, we must explore what God intended family to do. Only then will we have a clue about how to repair what has been broken. We start by looking at the traumas family never was intended to experience.

Take rejection, for instance. Its stark reality plays out in people's lives over and over. We see it on the playground where two arguing schoolmates taunt one another with angry words:

'I hate you.'

'I hated you *first.*' Even youngsters know how to protect themselves from rejection by rejecting others first.

Rejection is so fundamentally threatening to our psyche that we do almost anything to avoid it. Face it, we want to be wanted. Beyond our physical needs for food, water, air and shelter, we crave belonging and acceptance. We spend our entire lives searching for acceptance from others and for a place of belonging.

Is there a reason God has placed this yearning in our souls? How does our desire to be loved and accepted tie in with His master plan for us?

The answer is family. Our longing to be wanted and accepted is meant to be answered by the early and strong bonding with our parents. Children gain a sense of connection and interrelationship from those who love them. Our sense of belonging to something bigger than ourselves starts in family. Everyone has an intrinsic need to love and be loved. Family provides the means for meeting those basic human needs.

We learn how to feel about ourselves from what we observe in our family settings. Habits of the soul develop in family. Real improvement in our self-image comes only as we understand that the early part of our family drama may have been misdirected. Duane's mother coached him into behaviour patterns completely out of step with what God wanted for him. Likewise, Cindy and Gretchen were directed by their upbringing to play their roles inappropriately.

Acceptance and belonging are supposed to begin in family. If they do not, or if they are not developed adequately, children experience alienation. That alienation will haunt them throughout their lives.

A picture of alienation came to me one day while I prayed for a man in our church. I knew Eric was troubled and lonely, but I had not sensed the depths of his alienation. As I began to pray, God gave me a picture of a cosy mountain cabin late on a wintry afternoon when the sun had just gone down behind a pine forest. In my mind, I saw Eric slip from the trees and move towards the cabin. Eric shivered in the cold. He went to the window of the family room and stood there, looking in at all the people talking and laughing inside by the fire. The people in the cabin were the members of his family.

With that simple picture, the Lord alerted me to the core condition of rejection and alienation in Eric's life. 'Eric,' I told him,' you don't have to stay outside. You are welcome in here with us by the fire.' When he heard that, he wept because he had never known the power of family to secure him in warmth, acceptance and relationship. From his earliest days he was left out of love, left out of family acceptance and approval.

Although Eric hadn't told me about his childhood, I could tell he was never in real family. His family communicated to Eric that he belonged on the outside rather than on the inside. His parents never taught him to expect that people would be delighted to have him stop by to visit. He was neither welcomed nor accepted in the profound way God meant for family to secure a child.

Family has a life-force all its own, distinct from the individual members in it. It is the world in which those members live during early childhood, and out from which they venture as they grow older. The natural inner response of children is to want to be part of family, to join with others to form a whole.

Babies do not want to be left alone. Neither do children when they are hurting—unless they have been taught to keep their feelings to themselves. When children are afraid to share their emotions within the larger circle of family or if they are unable to do so because the family is broken, they experience the trauma of isolation.

Maybe the closest analogy to the power of family is the power of love. Though we may have difficulty quantifying love or tracing its origin and physiology, we know its potency. Like family, love isn't a thing. It is a power, a force, an irresistible movement that affects the way we think and feel. Love creates chemistry between a man and a woman. Love blinds us to some things in the ones we love, and enables us to see things in them that other people cannot see.

Like family, love changes our motivations and our level of willing vulnerability to another person. Love causes us to do things we would not do otherwise. Love is the reason we skip along a pavement without embarrassment, the reason we get butterflies, the reason we abandon a promising career to start a family. We can't explain these things any other way.

Like family, love is a relationship between people, defined by certain terms all its own. It is a state of existing conditions—about and for *us* rather than *me*—within which people live out their relationship. That is why we speak of being *in love* with someone.

Older couples who have been together for a long time often say of teenagers who think they are in love, 'They don't even know what love is.' There is more to love than emotion; more than physical intimacy. Love has a definition all its own. The same is true of family. Family as a force exists even before a couple marries. Family has meaning and power beyond what most people can imagine. Family is not only a physical description, it is powerfully spiritual.

What would happen if we understood and released the power of family so that it would touch our spouse and children beneficially? Something deep within their hearts would flourish. Our loved ones would not only be freed from many of the traumas caused by dysfunctional family, but they would be released to a life of great freedom in the world because of the delightful assurances they received from a healthy, functional family.

That is the power of family. It is waiting for us to engage.

2

Instructions and Fine Print

God designed family to bless us. When we do not do things His way, family becomes a curse rather than a blessing.

When family doesn't operate the way God intended, it almost always ends up broken. Failure to follow the instructions, or using the wrong set of instructions, inevitably leads to disaster. Why do we ignore or neglect what we *should* do in favour of what we *want* to do?

One answer is the absence of immediate consequences. For example, we know that to maintain good oral hygiene we must floss, brush twice a day and have regular dental checkups. But those things are a bother, so we put them off. Or we delay changing the battery in the smoke detector, figuring that a fire couldn't happen until after we replace it. One way or another, we all have a sense of personal immunity—imagining that we will be spared any ill-effects of our negligence.

Along with feeling that 'it will never happen to me', we develop another attitude that excuses our dysfunctions in life. This attitude—'I'll deal with that when it comes up'—convinces us that we will be able to handle future consequences. Call it overconfidence, it assumes that because we are smart, sincere, capable people, we can overcome problems when they appear.

Few of us give much thought to how we want our

families to be. Instead we content ourselves with identifying how we do not want them to be (usually, the way *we* were raised). We figure that when challenges in our family arise, we will magically be able to meet them, because 'we love each other.'

Yet students who don't read any of the assigned novels in a college literature class do not pass the final exam. Couples who fail to save early for their retirement are shocked to discover how little they can set aside when they begin to save at the age of fifty-two.

It is ironic that we give so little foresight and planning to something as powerful as family. We marry with such enthusiasm and optimism that irreconcilable differences with our spouse or children seem inconceivable.

The Pushchair Syndrome

Things usually end up as they were set up. The process produces the product. We see that vividly when we don't read the fine print in the instructions. Maybe we think that what we don't know can't hurt us.

We grow accustomed to our haphazard approach to life—even when we know it does not serve us (or others) well. We push ahead boldly and wrongly, almost daring anyone to insist that we do it properly, and readying ourselves to be frustrated if the outcome is not to our liking. I call this the *pushchair syndrome*.

Some years ago my Santa responsibilities required me to do one of my least-favourite activities: assembling parts and mechanical pieces into a gift. In this case, I had to put together a Cabbage Patch pushchair for my youngest daughter, Lorrel, who was then five.

How hard can it be to put together a doll's pushchair? I asked myself as I ripped open the box. Collin, who likes to put things together, watched eagerly as I dumped out four wheels, two axles and a handful of nuts and bolts. It seemed pretty obvious how they fitted together. Fifty minutes later I snapped the last non-removable end-cap into place. Smiling confidently, I stepped back to admire my handiwork and *oh no!* I'd put one of the rear wheels on backwards, making the pushchair lame. Collin didn't know whether to offer his help or to creep away as I pounded the pushchair in frustration. *Dumb wheel*, I fumed, as I whacked it with a hammer.

I never did get that end-cap off. The pretty little pushchair, now battered, minus some paint, and able only to limp along on three turning wheels, bore silent witness to my handiwork. When I see that pushchair in Lorrel's room, I must face why I had problems with it. First, I'm not mechanically inclined. Second, I'm not meticulous or steady. With a 'close enough' and a hastiness to get on with it, I ploughed through the assembly too quickly for quality craftsmanship.

The real root of my problem with those assemble-the-night-before-Christmas bikes, wagons and doll's pushchairs is my refusal to read the instructions. I'm so anxious to get things built that I merely scan the diagrams, look at the picture on the box and start grabbing parts. Of course, the instructions always begin with a sentence in bold type warning the assembler to *read all the instructions* before beginning assembly.

The *pushchair syndrome* starts with an excuse for not doing what I should do. The excuse usually comes from convenient self-analysis about what kind of person I am: *I'm not linear, so I won't read the instructions.* My self-analysis excuses me from doing what I really ought to do. And, I build in the self-defence mechanism of being a 'victim' of unreasonable expectations of others: *Anyone who wants me to follow the fine print in the instructions is asking me to do what I cannot do because of how I am.*

All of us are capable of excusing ourselves like that on many levels. A husband decides that he isn't the sort of person who shows emotion and affection, and blames his wife for expecting him to be articulate on Valentine's Day. After all, she should have known when she married him he wasn't that sort of guy. Or, he might like to escape from the office to a quiet and peaceful home. He doesn't care too much whether everything is spotless, he just wants somewhere to forget the worries of the office and relax. So when his wife reminds him not to wear his shoes on the new carpet, he yells at her. In his mind she deserves it. *After all,* he thinks to himself, *I can't be worried about a little dirt; I've been working hard all day and I need to relax.*

A wife may constantly complain to her friends about her husband. She doesn't mean to be disloyal, but what else can she do? He is so hard to live with, and she needs someone to unload her feelings to. Some people might consider what she says gossip or dishonouring to her husband, but she feels it's just her way of being open. She has always talked things out to determine what she really thinks. It's not her fault that she needs to vent. Her 'dumb' husband is just so difficult to understand. If he didn't do the things he does, she wouldn't need to talk out her marital problems with her friends.

Once one partner excuses and justifies his or her own behaviour—on the basis of self-analysis and what any 'reasonable' person would do—there is nothing left to do but to blame the other partner for whatever is wrong in the relationship.

What happens next? We feel stuck. Once we have set up a system to excuse our personal weaknesses and immaturities, we resist new ideas or alternative ways of handling situations. The other partner must take 'their share of the blame *first*', and the system becomes irreparable. We cease to look for ways to solve our problems together as *partners*, and settle into a semi-truce as *adversaries*. The terms we offer ourselves in that truce may be an affair, a new career, isolation, or more often than not, continual conflict. Once we've moved into the cycle of blame, we seldom stop and examine the real cause of the problem—our disregard for the correct construction of a family.

I often think of my pushchair-assembling experience. My natural response was to blame the instructions, the design, the wheel, the weather—anything. But in fact, *I* was the problem. I never gave the instructions more than a cursory glance. I should have read them thoroughly and done what they said.

Husbands, wives, parents and children get frustrated and fall into the *pushchair syndrome*. What we do incorrectly in family quickly becomes the fault of the 'dumb' family. We resent the way things turn out, and our disappointment turns to exasperation—and a desire to forget the whole thing.

We blame, in an attempt to salvage our pride. We extend the blame to include anything we think it will stick to: our job takes up too much time; we married too young; if only the children were younger or older; if we had a newer home, or different in-laws. Each of us, according to our original self-analysis and self-granted permission to do what we want, how we want, comes up with our own logic of blame.

Right or Righteous

Have you ever noticed how much our human nature wants to preserve our own rightness and shift the blame to something else? Yet blame is a dead-end street. We argue, blame or attack others from a position of self-righteousness. This leads to one of the most common pitfalls in relationships—believing that the goal is *being right*. We try to mask our efforts to win arguments by pretending we are trying to figure out who did what, or more correctly, who was wrong.

We imagine that by discovering who was wrong (a foregone conclusion), we will exonerate the right one (guess who?). We want to be right because we think that nothing else is required of us. If we are right, then the burden of correcting things naturally falls to the one who is wrong.

But being right is not the same as being righteous.

If the 'right' one simply waits for the 'wrong' one to come around and admit his or her error, the relationship has not been well served. Yes, it is important for the one who was wrong to acknowledge the mistake and sincerely apologise. But how do we act if we are right? The wrong thing to do with our 'rightness' is to act smugly or say, 'I told you so.' Or to use it as an excuse to do wrong ourselves.

Righteousness always seeks to preserve relationship through acts of forgiveness and mercy. Its goal is higher than figuring out who was right. God uses His righteousness for more than pointing a finger at our wrongness. He extends His righteousness into the midst of our unrighteousness and makes a way for us to change. Proving we are right is legalistic and self-congratulatory, and it usually makes us feel justified in our wrong attitudes (bitterness, unforgiveness, anger, scorn) towards others.

Jesus tells us the righteous response is to forgive and turn the other cheek.

Or, take a wife who emotionally threatens her husband when he disregards her opinions. She manipulates him with emotional or sexual blackmail. We all agree that is wrong.

The husband is frustrated, hurt and angry. Those feelings are valid, we think. But can you see the problem? Having been wronged by his wife, a husband can easily become wrong himself in his response by being resentful of her, or even coveting another man's wife. The feeling of moral superiority—'I am more right than you are'—tends to foster illegitimate attitudes and emotions that sabotage relationships.

Being righteous is different from being right.

Through my years of observing and talking with couples, I've noted four common ways people who are 'right' deal with blame and frustration in marriage:

1. **Reduced expectations.** One or both of the partners resign themselves to a ruined life that has been diminished by the other's failings. They develop an underlying martyrdom tainted with bitterness, yet falsely ennobled by self-congratulatory sacrifice.

2. **Compensating successes.** The couple individually pursues their own interests, pouring themselves into accomplishments, advancements and activities such as career, the children's education or sports, and civic or church involvement, to the detriment of the family.

3. **Emotional disengagement.** This can range from boredom to aloofness, from stilted conversations with a spouse, to fantasy involvements with others. To survive continuously unmet expectations, *all* expectations (and thereby all emotions but those of anger and bitterness) are cut off.

4. **Physical disengagement.** The couple stop touching (first affectionately then sexually), they walk in front of or behind the other (never together), they do things

separately, they meet only when necessary and finally, they separate.

Nora and Tom and Change

Nora and Tom experienced several of these symptoms—at least according to Nora. I'm not sure if Tom realised how perilously close he came to losing his wife. Perhaps Nora's despair and ambivalence were accentuated by the fact that Tom didn't know the Lord the way Nora did. He was as supportive of her churchgoing and beliefs as she was of his lack of attendance and beliefs—which is to say, through the years they had come to an uneasy truce.

To her credit, Nora treated her husband respectfully and was careful not to try converting Tom through clandestine manipulations. Actually, Nora's hope that Tom would open his heart to God and attend church with her was as low as her expectations for the rest of their relationship. She had lapsed into *reduced expectations*.

Bottom-line, Nora believed Tom had ruined her life. Not purposefully or maliciously, but steadily. Since Tom hadn't turned out to be the romantic image of the man she married, Nora had allowed little disappointments to become roots of bitterness. Before long she was tending a huge crop of unforgiveness, and that led her to *emotional disengagement* from Tom.

She contented herself with less from Tom—less affection, less understanding, less communication. And Nora's lowered expectations became a self-fulfilling prophecy.

Tom, too, had feelings of disappointment and *reduced expectations*, but he was not as able to articulate them. Besides, he was from the old school, and it would have been unseemly to complain about vague feelings when his wife was so obviously devoted to their children, their home and his physical needs. Nora's sense of duty, coupled with Tom's choice to keep providing for the family's physical needs, kept them from reaching the final and terminal state of *physical disengagement*.

Nora felt trapped and doomed. She had no hope of Tom ever changing enough to approach their relationship the way she needed him to. Strange though it may seem for her as a Christian, Nora concluded that a good marriage depended on luck leading her to a good man. And Tom persisted in trying to be a 'good' husband to a wife he hardly understood.

As I said earlier, the world provides us with many inadequate approaches to putting things right. Tom and Nora had read a lot of books. But they tried to head their marriage in two different directions. They were like two children, each intent on building his or her own project, but with not enough blocks to go around. Marriages do not come preassembled. They don't tumble out of the box all put together on the wedding day. They must be built. Couples must follow the instructions and the fine print.

One day, while praying for a friend who also had major relationship struggles, Nora received a simple revelation from God. It has changed her life and her marriage. Nora realised that she had blamed Tom for ruining her life. But now she saw that the *blame*, not Tom, was the culprit.

It impresses me that the beginning of Jesus' good news for a broken world is repentance. The gospel of Mark tells us that John the Baptist proclaimed the coming good news with a call for people to repent—which literally means to change our minds. To reconsider. To come to different conclusions than the ones that have brought us to where we are. Repentance stays focused on me and the sin that crouches at the door of opportunity in my life. This does not mean that others have no sin. It just means that sin's desire is for me, and I must master its attempt to draw me to wrong conclusions (Gen. 4:7).

Nora's conclusion about Tom and their marriage had come to accusations. In her mind, he was emotionally insensitive and disappointing, and the marriage was doomed. God showed her that her conclusion was wrong. Despite Tom's wrong, when God convicted her of having a blaming spirit, she repented and changed her mind.

Nora began by thanking God for her marriage and for Tom. Here's how she stopped blaming Tom for not meeting her expectations: First, *she chose to believe that God could give her a fulfilling and happy life, even if it wasn't how she expected.* Second, *she set out to meet Tom's expectations rather than have him meet hers.*

Nora still hopes one day Tom will answer her legitimate longings, but in the meantime, she can be content without having all her expectations met. Rather than lowering her expectations in a glum surrender to the inevitable, she has chosen not to blame. It was her blame that made her situation seem intolerable. Blame had acted like an emotional magnifying glass. When she stopped using blame to justify her own wrong attitudes, she was no longer tormented by thoughts of revenge. Nora's solution to her family problems—lowered expectations—hadn't worked. God's solution—repentance—did work.

The Wrong Set of Instructions

As I've already said, families can be broken (made dysfunctional) in many more ways than by divorce. In fact, long before divorce occurs, things go horribly wrong—usually in terms of unmet or unrealistic expectations. 'How hard can it be?' ruins not only pushchairs, but families.

Instead of learning what family was ultimately

designed to be, we tend to idealise a few characteristics of the 'perfect' family we want to have. We set out to build that family, reasonably confident that we know how to make a relationship work. We get married because we believe it will make us happy. We have children, believing we will be good parents and that our children will show us the appropriate love and appreciation for all we will do for them.

But do we really know what we're doing?

Designers create things to fit together in a certain way—things like pushchairs, cars, aeroplanes, appliances, furniture. And some people (not me) have a knack for 'seeing' how things are supposed to work. To the mechanically inclined, the toy, the engine or the cupboard rack assembly each has an obvious logic.

The problem is, there are few couples who are able to 'see' the logic of family. Most of us who haven't followed the instructions have ended up with things backwards and upside down. In fact, we do not even know how a fully functional family should work.

When we admit that we don't know, we realise that our solution—trying to build family any way other than according to the Manufacturer's design—will not work.

Those of us married long enough for the honeymoon to end realise that this relationship thing is more difficult than we thought. Or, more accurately, this family thing is different from what we thought. Romantic dreams, noble aspirations and idealised scenarios shrivel in the glare of life's day-to-day realities. When we add the broken experiences of our own upbringing to our vague notions about having a family (as though it were as easy as making babies or buying a hamster), we quickly find ourselves bewildered.

'But wait a minute,' you may say. 'I have read the

instructions—at least as much as anyone else I know. I watched my own parents, I've read some books, and we even went to a marriage and family counsellor.'

All those things may be helpful, and they demonstrate your sincerity and effort. Unfortunately not all the 'instructions' we read are correct. And false instructions can be deadly. Couples looking for advice for their relationships sometimes inadvertently breathe in harmful ideas and theories. I'll conclude this chapter with one such misleading idea that causes relationships to suffocate. Most of the advice we get about building a good marriage is based on relationship as a *contract*. But contracts cannot sustain a good family. Let's see why.

Contracts

In our culture, marriages are sometimes referred to as social contracts. And the newspapers are full of stories about famous, rich couples who sign prenuptial agreements, spelling out the terms of their relationship to one another after the marriage is over. Marriage was never meant to be a contract. That is why we equate weddings with rings and wedding bells, not blood tests and licences.

It feels odd to us when people sign prenuptial contracts. There is something cheap and mercenary about hammering out a contract with the person to whom you pledge your undying love.

At least that is what we think in the early stages of our relationship—before things have had a chance to go sour. When the reality of conflict, tight finances or differing priorities surfaces, many couples lapse into a contract mentality in dealing with their spouse.

More than we realise, the way we treat one another—especially in the context of family—results primarily from the basis upon which our relationship is established. When families have a contractual relationship, they end up judging one another's performance. We want to be sure our spouse is holding up his or her end of the deal because at the heart of every contract is what we call *the consideration*—the bargained-for exchange.

The consideration can be a physical item (money, goods, services, land), or it can be the exchange of *promises to perform* contractual obligations in the future: For example, I may promise to pay £150 in exchange for having my bike fixed, or a couple may promise to pay £230,000 upon close of escrow in exchange for the promise to convey a parcel of property free and clear of other encumbrances.

In the family setting, contractual considerations can take many forms. Perhaps a wife has implied, 'If you meet my emotional needs, I will be faithful to you,' or, 'If you apologise exactly the way I want you to then I will accept that apology.' Husbands might say to their wives, 'If you keep yourself and the house looking good, I won't find someone younger who can,' or, 'If you let me watch the game, I won't act angry and make you and the children miserable.'

Sonia and Bruce

Sonia and Bruce were in another one of their squabbles about their holiday when they came to see me. I had picked up enough of this running debate through the years as their pastor to know its cause—unmet contractual considerations. The issue was minor, really, but both parties had dug their heels in because they felt there was a principle involved.

There was.

Sonia was very close to her mother and two older sisters who lived in Arizona. Her idea of a great holiday was to spend it cooking and talking with them—like she had done for years before she and Bruce married. The kids would play with their cousins, and Bruce, well, he could find something to do . . .

Bruce liked his wife's family well enough, and he didn't mind visiting from time to time, but he loved to travel and see new places. Staying put in Arizona left him little satisfaction except for the brief trips he took by himself to explore the surrounding area.

This year he was putting his foot down; he was taking the family to British Columbia. And the fight was on.

The problem is, of course, that we do not normally tell each other about our contractual considerations before we get married. Most of the expectations are unspoken—until *after* the contract is signed. We don't even realise how many expectations we have of our spouse, much less the ones he or she has of us. We feel betrayed or taken advantage of when things don't go the way we thought they would. He gets upset that she spends so much time on the phone instead of with him; she feels cheated when he isn't as supportive of her as he should be.

No proposal of marriage, no acceptance of that proposal and no wedding vows—however detailed or lengthy—can ever communicate the specific terms and conditional expectations we unknowingly bring to marriage. A contract marriage is doomed from the outset. Every member of the family will fail to meet the conditions—not simply because those expectations were never discussed, but also because they are so numerous.

If you haven't agreed to all the terms of the contract, you have not accepted the contract at all. When your spouse expects something of you that you have not agreed to in your contract, you feel justified in not giving it to them. Conversely, when your spouse says, 'I do,' you imagine that they are saying yes to all your unspoken expectations. When they refuse to do what is expected of them in your version of the contract, you feel justified in your condemnation of them.

That is why, emotionally speaking, family members who want to cut off a relationship must prove to themselves that they are the *non-breaching* party; that is what blame and unforgiveness are all about. Husbands and wives justify divorce on the grounds that their expectations have not been met. If they had known it was going to be like this, they would never have got married. *I never agreed to this* is all a husband or wife needs to be convinced of in order to file for divorce. That is marriage and family by contract.

What is missing from *contract* marriage is flexibility for contingencies. Today more than ever we insist on individual rights and looking out for number one, but that won't work in family. Why? Because a contract is based on performance, and becomes invalid when one partner can no longer fulfil his or her part of the contract.

The husband's contract with his wife may include sexual satisfaction. But then along come the twins, and the new mum barely has energy to crawl into bed at night. So what happens? The husband feels ripped off: this isn't the kind of marriage he signed up for!

Or the wife may have married her husband in part because he was upwardly mobile. But then he becomes stressed out with his job and goes into depression, forcing him to take a less stressful, dead-end job. There goes his wife's status and the affluent lifestyle. She didn't bargain on that, and now instead of supporting her husband through a difficult time, she has to work through her anger and resentment.

Or what about the parents who have high social expectations for their children? They begin to notice that their eldest daughter is not at all popular with the other children. She is quiet and doesn't seem to need many friends. The parents find this humiliating, and their expectations are unmet.

A contract is useful when purchasing a car or a home, but it is poorly suited to cover the changing lives of fallible human beings. In the end, contract thinking is absolutely destructive to God's design for family.

We need something more encompassing, more generous and more forgiving to build our family relationships upon. But is there something more? Is there something deeper that points us towards what God had in mind, and explains why broken families have been so destructive to the human psyche? What should underlie the bonds of relationship in a family? If not a contract, what will protect us from being taken advantage of by other family members?

And what clues will this new understanding offer us as we raise our own families? I'm not talking about another how-to approach. No, much deeper than that, I am talking about what's in the heart of God for His children—His gift of family.

3

What God Has Joined

Everyone wants a good family. We rate our family on a scale of 'horrific' to 'great', depending on how close we are to our parents or siblings, how supportive our family is of us and so on. We base our evaluation not so much on the physical particulars of our family as on how we *feel* about it. That internal evaluation of family unconsciously answers for us the question, 'How has my family influenced me?'

Family affects us. More so even than what individual family members do, family as a whole impacts us profoundly. We know how comfortable we are in our family, how welcome we feel there and whether or not it seems safe.

We also intuitively know what our family thinks about us. Its attitude towards us is communicated in a thousand ways—subtle and not so subtle. Somehow, we know what we are to our family. And whether we admit it or not, it matters to us what our family thinks about us.

Most of us can attest to the influence our families have had on us even years after we have left home. In fact, family is so powerful that even what happened generations ago still shapes us. Our roots go deep. Generational influences affect our lives today. Why? Because we are bound together with our family in a relationship that transcends the physical. Family is more than physical relationship; it is a spiritual entity.

51

The Bible refers to our relationship with God in family terms—He is our Father; we are the children of God. God intended family to be the most potent connection between people. He instilled it with a life force, a unique character and authority for our lives.

God designed family to be more than two consenting adults with children. When we are born into the family of God, we come into a pre-existing relationship. We belong to and share in something spiritual. God arranged His people into families and tribes—descendants of the sons of Isaac. The New Testament opens with these words: 'A record of the genealogy of Jesus Christ the son of David, the son of Abraham.' It is a book about family. God visits both blessings and punishments upon the descendants of people unto the third and fourth generations. Clearly, family is important to God.

What is this thing called family and why is it so important to God and to us? What is it we wish we had when we look back at the family from which we came? And what is it that we long to provide for our children?

Family Covenant

The primary meaning of family, and the secret of its potency to affect people their whole lives, is found in an old-sounding word called *covenant*. What we are crying for in family is covenant. Although the term may conjure up images of dusty books and rolled parchments, we must understand the notion of covenant if we are to grasp what has gone wrong in our families.

To gain a fresh understanding of covenant, let's look at the concept in everyday life. Most people vaguely associate the term with Sunday-school stories of God setting a rainbow in the sky after the flood to remind us of His promise not to flood the world again. Or perhaps, we remember hearing Jesus' words read by our pastor during communion: 'This cup is the new covenant in my blood.' For most of us, these and other biblical images connect covenant with something spiritual and sacred.

But covenants are also functional and down-to-earth. For instance, the League of Nations (the forerunner of today's United Nations) operated under what was called *The Covenant of the League of Nations*—a chartered agreement about the principles and practices around which those nations could come together. The agreement established a relationship between nations, based on a spirit of goodwill and peace.

To make covenant more current, think about a condominium complex.[1] Most homeowner's associations—which you automatically join when you buy a condominium—are based on what is called *Covenants, Conditions and Restrictions* (CCR). This document covers such things as height restrictions, uses of common ground or procedures for reconciling grievances within the association. A CCR is an example of a covenant that 'runs with the land'—meaning it goes with the territory and is not open to negotiation like items in a contract may be.

No matter who buys the condominium, or how many owners it has through the years, the CCR remains unchanged. It is called a covenant because of its permanence and because it is an established part of the relationship, rather than a negotiated and accepted offer of terms *for* the relationship. Yet even in something as mundane as a CCR, you can sense the importance of a covenant. People know not to mess with it or to try to subvert it to their own purposes. It is supposed to be *sacred—set apart* from normal

---

1. A condominium in the USA and Canada is an apartment building in which each apartment is individually wholly owned, while common areas are jointly owned.

squabbles and *entitled to the highest* respect from all parties. The purpose of a CCR, like all covenants, is to ensure peace, unity and mutual benefit for all covenant members.

Covenant Is Not Contract

Covenant spells out the basis for and the nature of a long-term relationship between people—a basis unlike that of a contract. Covenants are promises of how one party will always treat the other.

Covenants are not contracts. Whenever people confuse the two, problems are sure to follow. Contracts are business documents, and usually involve the sale or transfer of commodities, services or property. Contracts deal with contingencies; covenants disregard them. Contracts are designed to protect the parties' rights; covenants protect the oaths between the parties. Contracts spell out conditions; covenants establish promises.

A contract implies that our rights and property must be protected from abuse, fraud or hostile aggression. Covenants, on the other hand, affirm trust. Contracts are made when trust isn't enough. Covenant is about promoting each other and thereby ensuring maximum advantage for both. The aim of a contract is to protect one's self—getting as many pieces of the pie as possible (by taking them away from the other parties). As you see, contracts and covenants don't work well together.

We cannot *make* a contract in the way we can *make* a covenant. Contracts require both parties to work out acceptable compromises; covenants, on the other hand, are one-sided offers of promise. Contracts are lengthy and filled with small print, hidden clauses and numerous contingencies. Covenants are bold, simple and straightforward.

Contracts are *written;* covenants are *vowed.* Contracts are *signed;* covenants are sworn.

A covenant simply declares: 'This is how things will always stand between us.' Made with an oath or promise, covenant assures relationship, indicating what we can always expect from the one making the covenant.

Can you see the implications for your marriage or family if it operated under freely-given promises of a covenant, not under the conditional expectations of a contract? 'For better or for worse' sums up covenant—'No matter what comes our way, I will be true to my vows to you.' A marriage *contract* lasts until expectations go unmet. A marriage *covenant* lasts all the days of your life.

Covenant is based not on what your spouse has or hasn't done, but on what you have said to your spouse. The only way to break your covenant is to break your word.

'Till death do us part' is more than poetry. It acknowledges the permanence of covenant in marriage. That is what family is intended to be: a safe, stable world defined and given boundaries by loving promises and sworn assurances.

Covenantal family promises lifelong relationships that can never be threatened by changing circumstances.

In later chapters, we will deal with abusive situations, where staying in relationship can be dangerous. But to develop a healthy sense of what God intended family covenant to be, we must begin by focusing on what God had in mind—not what human beings have done to violate His intentions. Covenant is the key to understanding family, as well as the missing piece for solving the puzzle of dysfunctional families.

God's Covenant

God invented covenant. He is the first covenant maker. Therefore, God's covenant with humankind tells us a great deal about the way family covenant is supposed to work.

Looking through the record of God's dealings with people, we see that He longs to establish covenant relationship with us. Though we often think of the Old Testament as a set of rules and regulations, it is much more than that. It is the drama of God actively pursuing people, to win them over and to enter into covenant with them. God has instituted covenants throughout history—with Adam and Eve, with Noah, with Abraham and Moses (the old covenants), and with believers in Jesus (the New Covenant).

The old covenants gave us glimpses of the total picture—all that God ultimately wanted for members of His family. But those covenants lost their effectiveness, largely because of humankind's repeated offences and covenant violations.

In the New Covenant, God offers us a way to deal with the inevitable violations we will commit against it. This is what makes the New Covenant better than all previous covenants. Jesus' 'one sacrifice for sins for all time' (Heb. 10:12) enables God to forgive us when we break our covenant with Him; our sins and our lawless deeds He vows to 'remember no more' (v. 17).

Covenants can be broken. But God's New Covenant is unbreakable—not because we become 'good enough' never to sin, but because the covenant is sustained by God's provision to forgive our sins. The terms of the covenant include forgiveness and a way to nullify the effects of our breaking it. God doesn't offer us a contract, because we could never hope to keep our part of the deal. Instead, He offers us a covenant that He sustains with His faithfulness and forgiveness. God makes His covenant with us a matter of public record because He fully intends to keep it.

Because covenant seeks to do good to others, forgiveness is critical. Without forgiveness, relationships will stall as we wait for the other person to respond to us first. We wait for our wife to get her act together sexually before we find the energy to build the shelves in the family-room she has wanted for so long. Or we wait for our husband to give up late-night football before we agree to write to his family. Often unconsciously, we keep our relationship stagnant by making our actions contingent on what our contract partner does first.

Human relationships are fragile. If we want them to live up to their potential, we need something more generous and more forgiving than a contract. That's why the biblical model for all deep and intimate relationships is covenant. Covenant makes clear our responsibilities. It asks questions of us before it asks questions of our spouse. It emphasises responsibility for our own behaviour, rather than judging the attitude or behaviour of our spouse or children. Contract is based on their performance; covenant is based on our commitment.

Marshall and Tony

Now that we have discussed the difference in covenant and contract, you may see new possibilities for your family, like Marshall did.

As I listened to Marshall's exuberance and newfound hope for his relationship with his fourteen-year-old stepson, Tony, I couldn't help but think of the soccer team I coach. Somewhere in the fifth or sixth week of the season, the Red-Tail Hawks suddenly *got it*. They passed the ball, maintained their positions and played believing they could affect the outcome of the game.

In a counselling session, Marshall *got it*, too.

He and Tony were always at odds. Tony got at Marshall through a combination of *make-me* defiance and *get-mum-to-come-between-us* manipulation. Marshall resorted to anger and *you-better-do-something-about-that-boy* ultimatums.

Negotiations between Marshall and Tony got off to a rough start because Tony resented having a new dad. Marshall hadn't spent much time building a relationship with Tony before marrying Paula. He figured, 'It will take time, but Tony will come to accept me—or he's out of here.' It wasn't long before the relational negotiations broke down completely, and neither Marshall nor Tony would agree to even a *contract* relationship.

Marshall was a Christian who sincerely wanted his family to work. Not having any other model himself (his own dad was too busy to do much with Marshall as a child), he lived by the Golden Rule in reverse: *treat others according to the way they treat you.* His relationship with Tony grew miserable. Give and take. Compromise and trade-off. Probation. Wait and see. Mistrust. Conflict. *Forget it.*

When Marshall grasped the notion of covenant, he realised that he had never offered it to Tony. Though he had agreed to love and cherish Paula, he never extended that provision to her son.

Marshall saw that he could interact and respond to Tony, rather than react to what Tony did or did not do. That didn't mean that Tony could do whatever he wanted. There were still requirements and rules in the household. But those rules did not offer Marshall and Tony any basis for relationship—only a basis for war or peace.

Marshall was eager to offer Tony covenant, and in doing so became eager to offer Tony love. Marshall began by asking Tony's forgiveness and by acknowledging how hard it must have been when Tony's father left. Marshall is concentrating on how God wants him to be to Tony, not on how he wants Tony to be to him.

It may give you hope as you read this book to realise that there is a different way to relate to your family than you ever imagined. For you, this book will explain what has gone wrong in your family. More importantly, the covenant model offers solutions and new options for your family future.

Sadly, some of you are in desperate family situations, facing spousal abuse or toxic relationships. When I speak of covenant being *permanent*, don't misinterpret it to mean that I am advising you to remain under threat of violence and acts of emotional cruelty.

You may have lived under the distortion, pressure and rejection of contract relationship for so long that you cannot bear the thought of staying where you are. This book will help you understand why dysfunctional family has so devastated you. Understanding is an important step in recovery.

Forgiveness

No matter how successful your family, we can all agree that we are not very good at covenants. We have broken our promises as surely as promises made to us have been broken.

Remember, the Lord's Prayer asks God to forgive us in the same way that we forgive others. Jesus warns us to take the log out of our own eye *before* we try to remove the speck from someone else's. Debt is contract. Forgiveness is covenant.

If we don't think our sin or our failure is as bad as another's, then it is unlikely that we will ever truly forgive them. We become self-righteous when we think contractually in our forgiveness. We say, 'Well, because you are not as good as me, I suppose I will have to forgive you again' or 'If you promise never to do this again, I will consider it.' That is not covenant. Family will become dysfunctional if based on that kind of thinking because family wasn't made to function based on contract.

This all ties back to the difference between being right and being righteous. The goal of covenant is to be righteous—to offer forgiveness and reconciliation. In contract thinking, I use my rights (rightness) to evaluate what is done to me: 'What is happening to our relationship is a consequence of what *you* have done wrong to me.

But with covenant, damage to the relationship can be contained and healed by my choice to forgive. So the real choice in family covenant is: what will I do with the wrong you have done to me? Will I let it go and preserve the covenant, or will I hold on to it and let it break the covenant?

Molly and Jeff

That was the choice Molly faced when she learned of her husband's multiple affairs during the first fifteen years of their marriage. Shortly after celebrating their eighteenth anniversary, Jeff confessed his infidelities. For three years, God had been rebuilding and restoring him to integrity. In culmination of the process, Jeff was led by the Lord to acknowledge his evil doings and to accept whatever consequences his wife would exact.

This was no flippant *oh-by-the-way* confession. Jeff was profoundly sickened by what he had done. He humbly told Molly that he had violated her, God and their marriage. He did not ask for mercy because he felt he deserved none.

Molly was devastated. It took several weeks for it all to sink in. Her world was shattered by Jeff's revelation. Molly's thoughts and emotions swirled about in confusion (*How could he?*), self-incrimination (*I should have been more responsive*), hatred (*I'll kill him for this*), and numbness. But through it all, one question kept coming back to her: *What should I do?*

No one could decide that for her. No one could tell her what to feel or what course of action to follow. I told her I would support her no matter what she decided—either to forgive, or to end the marriage. The Bible gives her freedom to do either; grace gives her strength to do either, as well. I told her to find the heart of God and to find His grace.

She did.

By God's grace, she forgave her husband and preserved their covenant as husband and wife.

Covenant is not a guarantee that our spouse will not disappoint us, or that our children will never misbehave. It is, instead, a promise to enter into a growing relationship. Therefore, we have to allow for failure, for misunderstanding, for false starts. Covenant is not a quick fix.

Rather than offer you quick fixes for your marriage and family, this book discusses fundamental foundations that must be realigned as we move from contract family to covenant family. This is not going to happen overnight. A covenant relationship is something to grow into, a star by which to plot your course. And of course, growth is never uniform; there are slow times and there are spurts. But God is a redeemer, and has promised to aid us in keeping our covenant.

The Power of Covenant

Covenant is not merely a legalistic requirement placed on unhappy wives to stay yoked to brutish husbands or on pestered husbands to remain under their wife's control. Rather than dominating or confining, covenant illuminates and liberates. The power of covenant returns things to their intended hope-filled and love-filled beginnings.

We have learned that a covenant is a relationship based on promises, not conditions. It is permanent and designed to benefit others rather than ourselves. Because the promises that establish the covenant are sworn in the sight of God, we are accountable to Him for how well we keep them. That is what makes a covenant. But what does the covenant do once it is established?

Covenant is a spiritual force—as gravity is a physical force. You may remember wondering why, if the world is round, the people on the bottom of the earth don't fall off. Covenant can be as mystifying to adults as the concept of gravity is to young children. Gravity isn't a material object; it's a force. Without gravity, elements of our physical existence (like water, chairs, toothpaste tubes and cars) would be tossed randomly together like ingredients in a bizarre mixed salad. Things would be a mess.

Gravity is good—unless we disregard or deny it. One of the men in our church told me his five-year-old son mistook cartoons for reality and leapt off a platform in the back garden in an effort to fly. The boy's bellyflop into the dirt opened a gash under his chin. The real world requires us to acknowledge gravity's force and to cooperate with it.

Just as there are laws that govern the physical world, so there are laws that govern the psycho-emotional world. Those laws explain how various forces work. Because we open ourselves up at such a deep level in covenant, when it is broken or violated, the emotional consequences are devastating.

One of the elements governing the psycho-emotional world is a built-in longing for meaningful connection with other people. Companionship, conversation, intimacy and friendship all stem from our innate desire for relationship. While most healthy people enjoy periods of solitude and privacy, those same people find it intolerable to be alone all the time. The feelings we have for our spouse or for our children go deeper than reason. Parents fiercely protective of their first baby demonstrate more than survival instinct. Our nurture and love are at least as *spiritual* as they are *instinctual.*

Our hearts want to touch another's heart, just as our hand wants to touch another's hand. Not all emotional attractions end in marriage, and not all companionships become covenants. But covenant is the direction towards which true relationships move. It is the highest form of connection.

The word *covenant*, like the word *convene*, stems from the French word *convenir*—literally 'to come together'. It implies something deeper than a mere partnership that must be renewed repeatedly or worked at to be maintained; instead the *union* of covenant already exists as a completed, irreversible fact.

Furthermore, covenant emphasises what can be done *together* that is not possible *alone.* A covenant has a creative, proactive dynamic to it. When a husband and wife come together physically, they can make a baby. Their joining leads to something they could never accomplish on their own without having come together.

By joining together, the covenant participants create something more significant than merely the sum of the parts, and they create something beyond themselves. Individual nations become a league of nations. A man and a woman become a family.

Once it is established, a covenant has three powers:

1. The power to create a new identity. When a man and woman enter the covenant of marriage, 'the two become one.' A new identity is created. As a couple in covenant, they are more than two separate individuals who live together. While still uniquely who they were before they were married, they are now both part of the growing relationship between them. Furthermore, children may come from that relationship, but those children are not the same thing as the parents or as the relationship. Covenant makes something *larger* than and creates possibilities for something *other than* the individuals in the covenant.

2. The power to affect generations to come. Covenant is like the genetic code of heredity, transmitting characteristics and traits from parents to children. This is why covenants are so often associated with inheritances and wills. Just as a will is the legal means by which possessions are passed down to surviving family members, covenant has a powerful force of transmitting psycho-emotional elements from generation to generation.

Without the factors of heredity, children would bear no resemblance to their parents or to their siblings. But when parents join together in the act of love, they create a unique genetic combination that becomes like a signature on the conceived child. What heredity is to the physical relationship between family members, covenant is to the psycho-spiritual relationship between them. It mirrors the traits and composition of that family's health or distortion. The Bible is full of examples and statements that link spiritual consequences to succeeding generations. Covenant has the power to transmit *good* to our children's children.

3. **The power to shape the personality of the covenant members.** The family we were born into—and whatever family we may choose by marriage—affects not only our children and grandchildren but also ourselves. For instance, a woman married for twenty-five years to a verbally abusive, unaffectionate man will turn out differently from a woman married to a gentle, loving man. Troubled in her teenage years by intense shyness and experiences of rejection in school, Jean will end up a different person by spending her life with Gregg. He is one of those rare men with few personal needs or agendas in his marriage other than to affirm and encourage his wife.

Family covenant enables parents to shape their children by sowing seeds for their future—seeds of kindness, understanding, sensitivity and selflessness. For instance, one family I know has a mildly impaired child whose abilities lag a few years behind his natural age. This child's older brothers, though widely different in personality, are remarkably similar in two ways: both boys are incredibly gentle in one-to-one situations, and they are both patient beyond their years. Being in a family, watching their parents interact with their younger brother, has shaped these brothers for the rest of their lives.

The power of covenant to shape the personality of the covenant members has, therefore, a hopefulness to it. Seeds sown today will one day produce a crop that will replace what now exists. We can sow new seeds in our children that will counteract negative ones previously sown. Because God is a redeemer and covenant is powerful, we can have hope that over time our spouse and our children will reap the benefit of what we sow.

What we want in family is what God designed family

to give us: security, unconditional love, a place to learn and grow, to experience acceptance, validation of our own unique personhood, a group of people to support and love us all the days of our lives. That is why our hearts ache from our family past, and why they long for our family future. All earthly families fall short of the ideal family; still, God invites us to enter into His design of covenant.

The personal implications for you throughout this book are profound and far-reaching. You may discover huge holes where your parents unknowingly overlooked aspects of the covenant or left them unattended. Little things will come to your mind. Your heart will lead you back to unresolved feelings, to leftover wrongdoings, and to why certain things your parents said or did have affected you so powerfully. Embracing covenant design will bring hope and healing to all your relationships, by helping you understand what went wrong, and by giving you practical ideas for how to do right to your spouse and children.

4

I Take You to Be

In the previous chapter we looked not only at ourselves, but at a hope for our family's future. Bad families can be turned around, but it won't happen unless we start doing those things that enhance covenant in our families. I am talking about having a plan for our lives. People who live life intentionally see how one act leads to another. They experience the joy of seeing something they planned today becoming a reality tomorrow.

The Bible calls this *sowing and reaping*—another of the spiritual laws that shape our lives. The similar worldly axiom goes like this: 'What goes around comes around.' The choices we make and the things we do in our family produce fruit through the years.

This is true of Howard and Mabel, both eighty-two, who recently celebrated their sixtieth wedding anniversary. Their hair is silver and their eyes sparkle. They are as spry and spirited as two fifteen-year-olds, and the way they talk and touch communicates how much they still love each other.

When asked the secret of such a long and happy marriage, Howard and Mabel give the same advice: 'Don't go to bed mad. Learn to laugh at yourself. Don't lose your love to gain your point. And hold hands a lot.' These cryptic pointers cannot contain all the wisdom Howard and Mabel have learned through their years together, but they do illustrate how we reap what we sow.

Looking back in your eighties is sometimes easier than looking ahead in your thirties. Hearing of couples who have been married for several decades inspires us. But sometimes it is difficult to imagine how they did it, because unconsciously we think a good family is a result of coincidence and luck—not a result of what we sow. It wasn't luck that created a happy marriage for Howard and Mabel. Instead, they chose to live a certain way with each other. Those little choices—to laugh, hold hands and resolve conflicts quickly—sustained their family and their love.

What we sow we reap. Bounty or blight. Blessings or curses.

Intentional Living

The problem with sowing is that we don't reap right away. After we prepare the soil, plant the seed and irrigate the field, we have to wait. It can seem as if all of our hard work has produced nothing. If we don't stay conscious of the time lag between sowing and reaping, we will be tempted to stop sowing. That is why the Bible says:

> Let us not become weary in doing good, for at the proper time we will reap a harvest if we do not give up (Gal. 6:9).

When you look at your family, you may feel discouraged:

> 'Bill and I have traded insults for so long, it has become a way of life.'

> 'I feel as if I've lost contact with my boys because it has been so many years since we really talked.'

> 'I've been so rebellious against my parents that I don't think they even want to see me again.'

These negative family situations are the consequence of choices made by family members. They are the crop of poisonous seeds planted by what was said, what was done in their home. What they planted has now borne poison fruit.

We don't intentionally plant destructive, ruinous seeds. We do not want to violate our family covenant or ruin our family. We didn't realise that withholding compliments from our children could damage them so. We didn't understand that being so busy with work at the office could lead to such feelings of estrangement with our wife. If only we had known that the way we talked to our husband made him want to escape our complaining.

The deadliest seeds are usually the most carelessly sown.

Is there a way to use this spiritual law of sowing and reaping to bring a blessing rather than a curse? I believe so. The power of family magnifies consequences for its members. In other words, the seeds that we sow within the covenant of family produce a greater harvest than those same seeds would if sown outside the family. This explains some of the dysfunctions in our life that have resulted from our family upbringing. But there is an even greater value to sowing and reaping in family: if we plant positive, constructive seeds in our relationships with our spouse and children, we *can expect* those seeds to multiply a harvest of good.

Covenant relationship does not happen overnight. People who get married thinking that they will have instant emotional intimacy with their spouse are going to be disappointed. Covenant is a progression—from individual to corporate, from self-centred to 'us-centred'.

The marriage ceremony is one part of the continuum.

When you enter marriage, you already have some history as a couple, and after marriage you have a future stretching ahead of you. We do not go into marriage as a complete and perfect person, and neither does our spouse. Making vows to each other on our wedding day, we accept the task of growing and of identifying with each other no matter what. Covenant may not be lived out perfectly in the beginning, but we can grow into it.

But growing into something so opposite to our nature requires intentionality and purposefulness. If we don't stay fixed on our destination, we will *unintentionally* get blown off course. We see a purposeful progression occur for people who live life intentionally. They know A connects to B, and how both are part of completing the process. These people have a bigger plan than is obvious in any one step they take. Perhaps a personal example will help illustrate what I mean by intentional living.

Not long ago, I experienced this amazing intentionality first-hand when I was at home recovering from the flu. My wife, Pamela, offered to reorganise my half of our desk drawers. In one of the drawers she came across a pair of winter gloves.

'Where's all the rest of your winter stuff?' she asked.

'In the drawer in my wardrobe.'

'Wouldn't you rather keep all your winter stuff together in one place?'

'Sure.' (I had never thought of that before.)

I didn't understand that Pamela had much larger plans in mind than cleaning out the five drawers in our desk. To her, the desk, then my wardrobe and hers, and the hall cupboard, all related to one another. What began about 9:45 in the morning didn't finish until a day and a half later. By the time it was over, even one bathroom had been reorganised.

Pamela persevered because she understood that every-thing had its place. It amazes me that she is always working on a larger plan. Everything relates to everything else. And it all fits together into a whole that is perfectly constructed. Because I lacked her understanding, I couldn't appreciate the significance of little things and their connection to each other.

French Operas

The same is true of our understanding of covenant. What we do not understand, we have a hard time appreciating.

I'll never forget the worst school field trip of my life—going with my class at the age of thirteen to see a French opera. I didn't appreciate the experience. I had no clue what was happening. Funny-looking people sang at each other in a language I could not understand. Until then, I had only heard sounds like that coming from a shower. I got sick from eating too many sweets, and that didn't add to my appreciation. From that day on, I decided opera had noth-ing to add to my life.

On the other hand, I appreciate golf, and it puzzles me that everyone isn't into it. There are so many exciting subtleties—all of which are lost on people who don't play the game. Some of my friends feel the same about baseball, although I cannot understand why. Talk about boring—baseball means nothing more to me than a chance to throw cholesterol concerns to the wind and have a couple of hot dogs.

We miss so much about art, music, mechanics, science, cooking, sports and ballet simply because we do not take the time to understand the complexities of their patterns and the steps of their design. It isn't that we do not want to appreciate them, but that we have no context with which to form an opinion about them. Most of us understand *contractual* relationships, but we will need help in learning to appreciate the design of *covenant*.

Thus far in our exploration of covenant, we have examined how it differs from contracts, how covenants are made and the power covenants have to imprint our psyches. One last aspect we will examine is how covenant was designed by God, the first covenant maker.

Everything with design is assembled sequentially. God made the earth in six days. Plays unfold in acts and scenes. Books build to a conclusion through chapters. If one segment is left out, the whole work fails to accomplish its goal. Family covenant is like that, although we are not used to thinking of family as a designed creation with particular steps and definite patterns.

Design and Elements of Covenant

There are four elements to covenant design. Each one leads to the next, in much the same way as parts of a wedding ceremony flow from one to the other, or a play proceeds from Act I to Act II.

Each of the four parts is critical to the meaning of the whole. Being in covenant is not like eating in a cafeteria, picking and choosing from among the food selections. A covenant is a whole, comprising parts that cannot be separated from one another.

We will deal with these elements individually later, but let me introduce them briefly. Every covenant has these four elements:

1. **Exchanging names.** Both sides in the covenant name themselves. On my wedding day I said, 'I, Daniel, take you, Pamela, to be my wedded wife.' I didn't need to remind myself of my bride's identity—we had dated for five

years! Even though I was a little nervous, I didn't have trouble remembering who I was either. Instead, those words were spoken because a covenant begins with identification. On my wedding day, I made a covenant with one specific person. I did not promise to be a good husband to 'someone,' or to share my material possessions with the first woman who asked. No, I promised to care for Pamela and to be the best husband to her I could be.

Not only that, but *I* chose to make the covenant. My father couldn't get up at my wedding and promise Pamela that I would do all in my power to be a good husband. And neither could Pamela's mother assure me that Pamela would do all she could to be a good wife to me. When it comes to covenant making and keeping, we must make up our own minds, and speak only for ourselves. By exchanging names, we commit ourselves to covenant.

2. **Rehearsing history.** Just as God desired to have relationship with us, covenant members also long for relationship. God yearned for His people before He entered into relationship with them. When we are dating, we want to be together all the time. We long to be joined in covenant relationship.

After the honeymoon, couples find that any problems they had before marriage are still there. That is why I tell couples there is nothing magical about the wedding ceremony or the rings. What your spouse has been is most likely what he or she will be. A covenant is not a New Year's resolution to act differently in the future, nor is it a Hallmark card filled with improbable promises to your spouse. Covenant says, 'I commit to keeping the promises I made.'

3. **Making vows.** The vow defines the terms of the covenant. Boldly and clearly, covenant participants speak

their commitment to the other. There are no conditions, no escape clauses. Covenant binds the participants to the promises, but also liberates them from the roller-coaster ride of conditional love.

Covenant protects a relationship. As we have seen, contract relationships are doomed to failure because of the conditions and expectations that each party brings to the relationship. Even unspoken, they become a laundry list of breaches of the contract. I must encase all the love I have for my wife and my children within covenant in order to keep it safe.

That is what God has done for us. His love for us is based not upon what we do or don't do, but upon the covenant He has made with each of us through Jesus Christ.

4. **Accepting consequences.** When honoured, vows and covenant powerfully magnify blessing in the lives of the covenant members. Conversely, if the covenant or its provisions are abused or violated, destructive curses and consequences are unleashed. Covenant is like electricity—it can light a lamp plugged into a socket, or electrocute a child who sticks a pin in the same socket. Covenant consequences—either for triumph or for trauma—are inherent to covenant.

As we will see later, this element of covenant is the most foreign to our natural thought process, yet it explains the pain and ruin stemming from dysfunctional families—familes that have been broken or were never based on covenant. Once covenant is agreed to, so are the consequences of either keeping or breaking that covenant. Without consequences there is no covenant.

To have a good family or to understand why the family we came from has affected us so, we must understand the unbelievable power of covenant. Each of our life-long relationships—with God, our spouse, our children—is meant to be lived in the context of covenant. Covenant relationship has a dynamic that can work for us and the ones we love. By identifying and exploring the principles of covenant, we can see the entire picture—and then develop those stable, secure, enriching and fulfilling relationships for which we yearn.

As we look at each of these covenant elements, we will see three things:

- How God incorporates these elements into His covenant with us.

- How these covenant parts can and should be lived out within the context of marriage and family.

- How violation of them will lead to the dysfuncton that is all too familiar to us and those we love. Let's begin by examining the first component of covenant design—exchanging names.

Exchanging Names—God's Covenant

Establishing covenant always begins by naming the individuals involved in the covenant. That is why God always names Himself in His covenant promises. He calls himself 'The Lord who heals you', 'The Lord your provider', 'I AM that I AM'. God establishes covenant with His people by identifying Himself particularly, then by identifying the people themselves. God doesn't make promises to nameless, unidentified people. He calls people by name.

A covenant's validity is tied to the integrity of who we are. When God gives us His name, He gives us the guarantee of Himself. Significantly, He gave us the name of His son, Jesus, to rescue and restore us. His name is above all names because He is Lord above all Lords.

God does not merchandise His covenant provisions in a wholesale catalogue. Covenant is not made to any and all takers. God's covenant was with Israel, not with the Philistines. This name-exchanging element of covenant explains why God deals differently with the nations (Gentiles) than with His own people (the Jews).

Individuals from other nations could participate in the Jews' covenant relationship with God. But in doing so, these Gentiles took upon themselves another identity; they became Jews by spiritual conversion instead of by physical conception. To benefit from God's promises, they had to become part of the people with whom God had established covenant. Without becoming a *new people*, the Gentiles would be excluded from the covenant.

Both groups of people—those born Jews and those converted to Judaism—were in relationship with God through covenant. God identified them as His people when He named them. They were 'marked' in response to Him. That is one of the main reasons for circumcision—removing the foreskin signified that these were God's people. It was something unique and particular to them alone.

Throughout the Bible, God refers to His people as the children of those with whom He made covenant: Abraham, Isaac and Jacob. Often, as well, we read of God's naming or renaming people as part of His covenant with them: Abram is called Abraham; Jacob becomes Israel; Simon is changed to Peter; and Saul becomes Paul.

Today, of course, God names His covenant with any who 'will call on the name' of Jesus. God's people become His people of covenant by (re)birth and conversion:

But you are a chosen people, a royal priesthood, a holy nation, a people belonging to God, that you may declare the praises of him who called you out of darkness into his wonderful light. Once you were not a people, but now you are the people of God; once you had not received mercy, but now you have received mercy (1 Pet. 2:9–10).

God's covenant remains constant and fixed on a people to whom He has given His name. The New Covenant fulfils the old covenant. The difference in the two covenants is that God's people are identified—by natural birth and obeying the law (the old covenant), or by supernatural birth and obeying the spirit (the New Covenant).

Exchanging Names—Marriage Covenant

We begin telling someone who we are by giving them our name. Though shared by other Steves, Lindas or Chesters, our name is profoundly private. We rarely think of ourselves by our own names. Yet when we think of others, their names encapsulate everything we know about them. A name is a symbol by which we identify people.

Since covenant is all about people—not things or services or performances—whatever will be true about the covenant will be the consequence of who and what the covenant makers are. For instance, people who have a tendency to boast—to make themselves out to be better than they are—will bring that to the relationship. Or people who find it impossible to admit they are wrong because they are so full of ego and pride will bring those traits to the relationship. Their actions, and not their name, mark their true identity. Thus, name exchanging is not a casual, trivial activity. In offering our name to another person, we are offering our *selves*.

This has implications for people who, though married, nevertheless act and think like singles. As a pastor, I often see 'married singles,' a phenomenon that occurs most frequently among people who don't marry until in their late twenties and early thirties. Having grown accustomed to being single, they continue to do what they want with their time and money without considering their partner. They have not yet given their total being to their partner; instead, they have tried to *add* marriage to their previous lifestyle. Covenant is not about adding and accumulating, it is about giving yourself away and relinquishing your hold on what you call your own.

Marriage covenant begins with name exchanging. All that follows the ceremony—the promises, the rings, the intimacies and the years of life together—is based on the two people exchanging names to identify themselves and one another.

By exchanging our names, Pamela and I pledged ourselves utterly to one another. Our covenant was ours to make. Our covenant will always be ours to keep. Covenant links our identities for the rest of our lives—for better or for worse. You can see how critical it is to know someone well before establishing covenant with him or her.

Gordon and Jeananne married when he was eighteen and she was barely seventeen. That was forty-four years ago, and both admit they had no idea what they were doing. I'll never forget what Jeananne said about their marriage:

Neither of us knew who we were. Our personalities were still forming. The man I married at seventeen was not the man I welcomed home from

*the Korean war three years later. He had changed
drastically. But so had I. Lucky for us, we liked who
the other had become.*

We are married only to the one with whom we
exchange our name. The marriage licence is valid only for
the two people whose names are on it. Completely exclu-
sive. I am not married to everyone who heard me speak my
marriage vows. I spoke them to one woman alone, to
Pamela.

Years ago, I heard of a young bride jilted a few days
before her wedding. For her own reasons, she went ahead
with the wedding without her intended groom. She ran an
ad in the local newspaper: 'Bride and wedding looking for
suitable groom. Send resumé and photo.'

A wedding ceremony and a marriage covenant are not
the same thing. One is only the cover of the book. The
other is the story.

Exchanging Names—Family Covenant

Children also enter family covenant by name. When a baby
is born or adopted into a family, the first thing the parents
do is name the child. Covenant cannot be made with
unidentified people. Without giving the child a name, parents cannot make covenant with him or her.

In the covenant of family, name giving is promise
giving to children—a promise of an identity for them. In
later chapters we will discuss how family gives children
their identity throughout their life-time, but the process
begins here with name giving.

Because I have never been a good speller, three of my
four children have uniquely spelled names. Pamela was
exhausted after each birth, so I was charged with filling in

the children's birth certificates. We had already agreed on their names (depending, of course on their gender), so all I had to do was write in the name. Thus, Hilary, Collin and Lorrel will forever have to correct the way people spell their names. Fortunately for Evan, our youngest, even I could not come up with an odd way of spelling his name.

A name makes a person unique. It enables the person to be known, to be separated from the crowd. Every person longs to be special, to have his or her own life lived in relationship with others. When parents give children names, they are, in effect, choosing those children. A name pulls a child from a blurred existence into focused relationship. Without a name, we have no identity, no distinctives. Naming is an integral part of the spiritual power of covenant to give people a reference point for starting life.

Covenant name giving explains why some mothers can so easily abort their unborn children. Without a name, the foetus remains a 'thing' in the mother's mind, not a person. The mother can disregard her natural instincts to preserve her child's life because she does not acknowledge the foetus as hers—she has established no covenant with the baby. Not giving the baby a name is her intuitive way of giving her baby no promises.

Think about nicknames. Nicknames (not name calling) acknowledge a special relationship between people. Affectionate names communicate an intimacy not shared with everyone else. Meaningful relationships usually evolve unique expressions of addressing one another. For husband and wife, they range from the usual *love*, to the formal *sweetheart*, to the unique *toots*, to the unintelligible *mai*.

I have several special names for my kids—all of them non-sensical and arbitrary. That is the point—the names themselves are blank, without meaning. Hilary was

Pumpkin as a toddler, *Hilwey* as a little girl, and now she is *Hildeberry*. Collin is alternately *Bud* and a heavy French-accented *Co-lawn*. Lorrel's names seem to centre around the vowel O: she answers to *Yo*, *Yodeeoo*, *Lo* and *Yodes*. And somehow, Evan elicits sch-type nicknames: *Schmugs*, *Schmai* and *Schmevan*.

The children I love fill out their names and give me, their father, additional terms with which to focus my love on them. Nicknames are like photographs. Pamela and I take pictures of our kids so our hearts can overflow every time we look at them. Naming is love giving. Naming is promise giving. Covenants require names.

Exchanging Names—Dysfuncional Family

Beginning covenant with an exchange of names stresses the uniqueness of the people in the covenant. People do not get lost in real covenant; in fact, in family the way God meant it to be, each member's distinct personhood is accentuated and promoted.

Covenant bonds people together, but it does not force them to sacrifice their personhood to be part of the whole. Dysfunctional families can overwhelm individual personalities or uniquenesses. For example, a father who sexually abuses his daughter has denied who she is; she has ceased to be his daughter and has become, instead, an impersonalised object to use. Likewise, a mother whose anger makes everyone tiptoe around has established her personhood as the most dominant force in the family. Her 'freedom' to act as she wants imprisons everyone else. That violates covenant.

Researchers have noted that in dysfunctional families, family members are not encouraged or even allowed to be themselves. They are burdened with a caricature, a part in some grim domestic drama. Without opportunity to explore and express the unique subtleties of their own personhood, children in distorted families become something other (not even some*one* other) than who they really are.

In God's concept of family, personalities are never obscured. Instead, real family promotes the fullest expression of each family member's self. Ridicule, unfavourable comparisons, name calling and shaming statements that begin with 'You are so . . .' find no place in real family because they violate the first element of covenant—exchanging names and promoting the personhood of *all* covenant members.

People who come from dysfunctional families—most of us—expend huge amounts of emotional energy searching for their true selves. They experiment with various lifestyles, dress styles, moral codes, politics—all in the hopes of establishing an identity that either was never established or was taken away from them by a family that violated the first element of covenant.

Jenny and Larry

Several years ago I counselled a woman who grew up as the oldest daughter in an alcoholic home. Jenny was bright, energetic and on top of the world. Nothing got her down, and everyone wanted to be around her. She brightened every social function, and she could draw the best reactions out of young children and old folks alike.

The first hint of trouble came in the emotional fatigue she felt towards her husband, Larry. Jenny was tired of him, not in the sense of wanting another man, just tired of how he was. Contemplating life alone, without him, gave her a sense of great rest.

Larry had his own issues that would tire any wife. But not the way Jenny tired, so abruptly and hopelessly. When I prayed with her, God showed me a picture of an old oak beam that had been twisted and bowed by bearing up under too heavy a load. I shared the picture with her, and told her I knew it had something to do with how she was raised. Almost immediately, she began to cry tears of healing.

The heavy load had been her father and her family. She became the 'fixer' in her dysfunctional family and carried the burden of that role into her own marriage. God healed her, and even though Larry still has some issues he is working through, both have great hope for their future.

And Jenny still is a delight to all who know her.

In true covenant family *who* you are is always primary. Family promotes individuals and helps them express themselves. It never represses their individuality. In dysfunctional families, too much attention is given to the whole family or to one or two of its members. Affection and delight are spread unevenly, or not expressed at all.

Distorted families emphasise what you do more than who you are; they talk more about your outside appearance than about what is going on inside of you. The distinctions parents make between their children are blurred, or they are made on the basis of performance, not personhood. Giving names actually gives meaning, and children who are identified by their parents over and over again—spoken to and related to individually—will never suffer the trauma of identity crises.

The power of the first element of covenant in true family—exchanging names—is how it makes us feel special, chosen and singled out for affections. More than just saying, 'I love you,' it exclaims, '*You* are the one I love.'

5
No Place for Strangers

Our exploration of covenant—what God intended family to be—sheds light on why so many families are dysfunctional. In one way or another all dysfunctional families violate or ignore the elements of covenant. Rarely are those violations intentional; it's just that the way we know how to relate isn't the way God intended for us.

As we have already learned, covenant has four parts to it, like the movements of a symphony. The first element of covenant is *name exchanging*. In this chapter we will look at how true covenant leads to a second element—*rehearsing the history of the relationship with one another*.

It is one thing to know someone's name; it is altogether another thing to know about them—what they are like, how they react, what is important to them. The only way to know such things about someone is to have a history with them. Based on how you have seen a person behave before, you know how she or he is likely to behave in the future.

That is why the second critical element of covenant is rehearsing history. True covenant not only names the parties involved; it also reviews the particulars of the relationship between them. It spells out what things have been like between them. It says, 'You know me and what I am like. As I *have been* to you, I *will be* to you.'

Outlining what has gone on before between the

people of the covenant legitimises and establishes what will go on between them in the future. A history of sights and sounds experienced, of places visited together, of emotions and circumstances explored hand-in-hand—this is what we must have to make covenant with someone.

We make contracts with people with whom we have no assuring history; either they are strangers, or their past dealings with us convince us they may take advantage of us in the future. Contracts secure the future with stipulations, clauses and conditions. These give us a recourse—a means of recovering damages the other party will probably cause.

Covenants secure the future with perpetuity, not with provisions. That is, people in them continue to perform and act as they have in the past. A *perpetual* annuity is a specified and fixed sum of money paid (usually yearly) to someone for the rest of his or her life. It comes regardless of other factors and considerations. That is the essence of covenant: once established, it continues to perform, without change, into the future.

History and Landmarks

As a young boy, I loved the dusty scent of sagebrush on a hot summer day. All these years later, one whiff of its heavy, earthy smell and I am transported to a time when I romped through the high desert mountains, where I grew up, north of Los Angeles.

My favourite pastime was to take my bow and three arrows across the alfalfa field and into those mountains that were dotted with yucca bushes, chaparral and several varieties of sagebrush. I shot at everything—birds, rabbits, even imaginary foes.

I spent hours roaming up and over the irregular mountain ridges, winding through the sage and chaparral on rabbit paths. For an eleven-year-old, I developed a good sense of direction amid the tiny valleys that resembled each other so closely.

Only once did I come close to really getting lost—the problem was landmarks. There weren't many, because the terrain was so monotonous. Each hillside looked like the next, and even the horizon looked much the same in all directions.

But I had a history with my mountains and valleys.

I knew the great places to jump off, the steep slopes that were fun to run down but a pain to climb up, which way the quail ran and which scrub oak they always came to at dusk, the spot near the top of one hill where several trap-door spiders made their homes. No way could I get lost in my hills. I knew them from all the hours I had spent on them; and, I liked to think, they knew me. My hills felt familiar to me because of our shared history.

The problem came when, on a long excursion with my friend Mike, I left the familiarity of my valleys and hill-crests. It was a Saturday, and we had each packed a lunch, a flask and more than our usual number of arrows. We were going exploring.

I remember the excitement of pushing up one more hillside to see the next valley. We weren't looking for any-thing specific, we just wanted to see what we hadn't seen before. Panting and sweating, we clambered through the sage, around the yucca, up one hill and down another, always alert to shoot at any movement.

Eventually, we grew tired of missing birds and losing arrows. We concluded that the next valley probably wasn't worth the climb out of the one we were in. It was time to go home.

Oops . . .

Obviously, I lived to tell about nearly being lost forever! Mike and I found an alfalfa field and a dirt road, and followed it. Without realising it, we had walked four miles to the other side of the mountain range. When the dirt road finally came out to a place we recognised, we could not believe how far from home we had wandered.

Something like that can happen in families. People get lost because they lose sight of their history together. They wander away like foolish boys who imagine that the unknown offers more than the hills and valleys with which they are already familiar.

Or, even worse, some people try to make a family out of relationships that have no history to them. Family is no place for strangers. Just as we cannot make a covenant with people whose names we do not know, neither can we make covenant with people with whom we share no history. Covenants require a past to guarantee the future.

Rehearsing History —God's Covenant

Before we look at how the dysfunctional family violates this second aspect of true covenant—rehearsing history—let us examine how God establishes covenant. Over and over, God identifies Himself by saying to His people, 'I am the God of your fathers . . . ' He then relates things He has done—His history with them. God didn't come lately on the scene, in the mood for a quick, easy relationship. He doesn't view covenant relationship as an experiment.

Besides giving us His name, God establishes His credentials for covenant. Relating the history of the relationship reminds us that He has shown Himself in the past to be loving and merciful. History with His people proves His character and makes the covenant He offers believable.

Telling our children stories of God's wonderful works

gives them an historical context for covenant with Him. Believing that God is good and that He intervened in history on behalf of His people, these children find it easier to welcome covenant with God than do children who grow up in homes where God's name is used mostly in vain.

Covenant maps out familiar territory within which people can be safe and secure to enjoy life. Like my connection to my valleys and hills north of Los Angeles, having a history with someone lets you know what to expect. In all the covenants God established, He identified Himself not only by name, but also by rehearsing His history with the people. God is not moody, whimsical or erratic. As He has been, He will always be. He wants us to know Him, and by knowing Him to be assured of how He will act in any situation.

The Bible tells us there is no 'shifting shadow with God'—there is 'no variation' in Him, nor do His dealings with us change from day to day (See James 1:17 NASB). In the same way, we find covenant assurance perpetuity and continuity—in the fact that 'Jesus Christ is the same yesterday and today and forever' (Heb. 13:8).

The first covenant God established with humankind made a place for Adam and Eve to live. Eden, with its definite borders and landmarks, became a familiar place, like the mountains were to Mike and me. God told Adam and Eve what they were allowed to do and what they could expect. In fact, God's pattern of dealing with them was so familiar that they anticipated His response to their violation of the covenant. They realised they had forever changed things by violating their covenant with Him.

Most of us focus on Adam and Eve's failure. We see their sin and the deadly consequence of their covenant violation—they were expelled from the Garden of Eden and they ultimately faced death. But if we look at the covenant itself, we gain insight into the second element of covenant. Though covenant violation will radically change our future, the real purpose of covenant is to map out a place of certainty. Covenant removes doubt because it fixes us in a place of psycho-emotional familiarity. That is analogous to the garden where God set Adam and Eve. If they had not broken the covenant, they would still live there, essentially unchanged.

Rehearsing History—Marriage Covenant

'For this reason'—to establish covenant with his wife—'a man will leave his father and mother . . . ' (Gen. 2:24). Not only did this first marriage covenant begin with man naming woman, it also acknowledged their shared history. God took one of Adam's ribs, and out of it fashioned Eve. They were 'bone of bone; flesh of flesh'. This commonality and shared experience set the stage for legitimate covenant between Adam and Eve. It made them suitable for one another.

Likewise, a history of relationship together was the basis for Pamela and me to enter into covenant with each other. Though we married young (at twenty), we had dated steadily for five years and knew each other well. People don't have to know each other that long before they marry, but without some history, the covenant of marriage is more a wish than an oath.

At least some history—meaningful history that reveals our character—is necessary for legitimate marriage covenant. Because we met, did things together and shared many experiences, Pamela and I were sure we could *promise* a lifetime of constant love to each other. We had already found out about each other in the years prior to our wedding day.

With a shared history and a covenant, husband and wife legitimately join their bodies in an expression of determined oneness and total intimacy. It is no accident of language that a couple who join together sexually are said to 'know' each other. Sexual intimacy has a spiritual potency to it that can meld two people together. But from the beginning of true family covenant, sexual union is the *postscript*, not the *prelude*, to becoming one through the shared history of the relationship.

The physical expression of the marriage covenant is meant to mirror the covenant itself: 'Because I now know who you really are, I am ready to give myself in covenant union to you.' It is perverse and self-serving for a couple to start with this joining mark of marriage covenant and then see if they can get to know each other and get along. This is the critical flaw of living together before marriage. 'History' that takes place *after* establishing sexual intimacy isn't the kind that leads to true covenant.

Certain parts of our soul and our body were meant to be touched only within the safety and permanence of an established covenant relationship. Shared history secures the walls that protect shared intimacies between husband and wife. Remember, the purpose for covenant is to secure relationship between people, for ever. Covenants are not made in haste, nor are they used to *begin* intimacy. They are made to preserve both the boundaries and the blessings of having been together at one level of relationship, and now wanting to move to a higher, permanent level.

Rehearsing History—Family Covenant

Equally as important as the names we give our children is

our history with them. I believe God arranged for children to be born nine months after they're conceived to enable parents to have history with them *before* covenant is established. Any mum who has carried a child in her womb knows the amazing bonding that develops with her baby. The two of them go places together; mother talks to and confides in baby; they feel each other both emotionally and physically. When baby is born, he or she is not a stranger. There is already enough history to surround the baby with love and with family covenant.

Notice that much of the history mum and dad have with their unborn child consists of things they do for the baby. They paint the nursery and get it ready; they buy clothes; they adapt their schedules; and they arrange for nappy service. This gives us a clue about meaningful covenant history.

Not just *any* kind of history with someone will pave the way for covenant. The one who initiates covenant— God with us, us with our children—legitimately does so only on the basis of what he or she has done for the other. Only a giver and a care provider can offer true covenant. Takers and self-servers are impostors at covenant. Self-interest is one of the surest signs of a dysfunctional covenant. Self-interest offers only contracts, never true covenant.

It will be a long time before the unborn baby can serve the parents. No matter, because the established pattern of shared history means that covenant can be established. Having a history of serving gives us the means to covenant with our children. Covenant essentially says, 'On the basis of how I have been towards you—the way I have loved you and served you—I offer a lifetime of the same.'

In the same way, parents who adopt a child develop a

history with their child before he or she comes into their family covenant. Most adoptive parents long for a child for years, and each time they receive a call or visit with an adoption official, they hope 'maybe this time'. This anticipation is akin to that experienced by couples who 'try to have a baby'—each time, they wonder if the child will be conceived.

You see, *longing* for a child is a history strong enough to sustain covenant. What parents (either adoptive or natural) long for is someone to love, someone to serve. Parents who have a child only out of some self-satisfying need of their own are illegitimate parents. Covenant comes only after a longing to serve, not to be served, has been established.

Rehearsing History—Dysfunctional Families

This explains the tragedy of families that never become what God intended. A child who has not been longed for by parents is born *outside* of covenant. I want to clarify the distinction between *unplanned* children (our first and fourth) and unwanted children. Being surprised by the joy of 'we are going to have a baby' is not the same as being unhappy about having one. The attitude of the parents determines both the extent and the nature of the history leading to covenant. When true family covenant exists between husband and wife, there are no unwanted babies. Covenant already exists, and all babies, all family, are always safe within it.

Abortions are often motivated by parents' perceived inability to serve their baby. In the case of incest or rape, a mother may doubt that she can overcome her trauma to love and serve the child she has conceived. Financially overwhelmed parents might see no hope of providing for and serving their child. We should understand these fears, and address fearful parents with love and hope.

Sometimes abortions are simply a consequence of parents' unwillingness to serve their unborn babies. These parents are not afraid that they can not serve; they are determined that they will not serve at the expense of themselves, their career or their personal fulfilment.

Covenant is an offer of aid, support, nurture and care. Covenant always costs the covenant maker—a lot. Mothers and fathers who do not want to make the personal sacrifice it takes to offer covenant to a child in the womb are not in a true family themselves.

We cannot establish covenant with strangers. Knowing someone and having history with them is the whole reason for and the grounds of the covenant. In dysfunctional families, people are strangers to one another. Family members hide their true feelings and thoughts. They fear exposure and being known. They wear masks to cope. Families that discourage or prevent true intimacy disallow covenant and thereby cease to be family.

Barbara and Skip

Barbara and Skip came to see me in the midst of a fight— their latest. It centred around her complaint that he controlled (or rejected) her and his complaint that she responded to him as if he was the ghost of her father.

I've seen many of these *you're-pushing-me-away* wars. Sometimes a husband will tell his wife to stop treating him like his mother did, and a wife may wish her husband was more like her father. Our parents pop up in the strangest places. Echoes of their voices—reminders of how they dealt with us when we had the mumps or when we brought home our first 'D' on a report card—keep calling out to us with confusing, emotional consequences. Marriage fights are sometimes battles with our parents and the families in which we grew up, rather than with our spouse.

Barbara's parents divorced after years of mutual manipulation. Theirs was a perverse cooperation, a sick kind of co-dependency with simple rules for *getting along* while hating each other. Both of them were martyrs who waged relentless war on each other. When they suffered even the smallest defeat, they would escape to their separate pursuits. His was business (he became quite wealthy). Hers was church (she became quite religious).

If Barbara's parents had been childless, the damage from their war game would have been *contained* rather than *collateral*. Unfortunately, one of the acceptable hazards of war is that innocent civilians—those who never enlisted in the fight—are affected. Barbara and her sister were emotionally maimed by the constant salvos fired by their parents. The hostility of the parents had an ugly spillover into the lives of their daughters.

Barbara's father and mother did their best to draw their daughters into their respective 'safe zones' of finance and liturgy. Barbara's father offered her the carnal and fleshly keys to his world of business; her mother wanted Barbara to follow her into the spooky and bizarre world of religiosity. Barbara's father gave her anything she wanted—drugs, parties, the best clothes and a career in the record business. But all that *freedom* came with a price: her father's control. She could have anything she wanted as long as she did what he wanted her to. What he wanted was for her to reject her mother. Control and rejection went hand-in-hand in the family Barbara grew up in.

Barbara's mother played the same game. Instead of offering financial incentives, she offered her daughter spiritual counsel—a strange mixture of world-conspiracy beliefs, mysticism in the guise of theology and fear. Again, the price for spiritual security and freedom for Barbara was identifying her father as a reprobate beyond hope of salvation.

Both her father and mother tried to control Barbara. Ultimately, if she didn't do what each of them wanted (reject the other parent), they threatened to disown (reject) her financially and spiritually.

Control and rejection.

Barbara's history with her family became dysfunctional. But thanks to covenant healing, a new history is possible with her husband.

Even those not married can receive ample healing by meaningful history with key people God brings into their lives. And of course, history with God forms the backdrop for all recovery. The challenge to Barbara's husband, Skip, is to avoid using control or rejection as Barbara's family did, something he is doing fairly well.

Barbara unknowingly *expects* her future to be like her past. It is up to Skip to make her future a promise of his history with her, rather than her parent's history with her. That will not be easy. The past profoundly influences our future; it tells us what to expect from others, and how to behave towards others. The lasting effect that her family upbringing has had on Barbara proves the power of the second element of covenant. Shared history shapes our future. Although her family history has had a negative influence on Barbara, she and Skip can harness the same power of history to shape a brighter future with each other.

Covenant offers Skip what he needs to give Barbara the hope and power to recover from her dysfunctional upbringing. Skip is discovering that the more he releases and promotes Barbara—without any strings attached—the more she flourishes. Creating a new shared history creates a new future for them both.

Being Together for Tomorrow's Sake

Dysfunctional family members do not long for each other. They do not particularly look forward to seeing each other, and even with the passage of days, weeks or years, they do not really miss each other. Families that do not like spending time together are usually dysfunctional.

The members of such families learned that their unique experiences are uninteresting to others in the family (most notably the parents). When we share what happens to us, we actually share ourselves. Thus, a family who ignores or ridicules children when they talk about their day becomes less of what family was meant to be.

Healthy families talk a lot about past incidents—holidays, ball games, when Mary lost her first tooth. Family members tell stories about one another and 'the time when . . . ' Children love to be told about themselves—what they were like as 'little kids', funny things they used to say, the house they lived in when they were small.

Members of functional families love one another as much as or more than themselves. They serve each other and they treat the others as they would like to be treated. Mum or Dad have no more right to get angry than anyone else. Within the bonds of love, true identity of family members begins to emerge in shared history.

Intuitively we sense the danger in 'drifting apart' and 'not knowing what is going on' with family members. When husband and wife complain that 'the relationship isn't developing any more,' they acknowledge they are no longer creating a common history with each other.

Sometimes, couples will hide their drifting and lack of relationship by concentrating on good sex. That won't work for long. Making love isn't accomplished in bed. Love is 'made' by creating ongoing, intimate history with each other.

In a dysfunctional family, members are aware of their isolation and separateness from the rest of the family. Instead of teaching *we* and *us*, dysfunctional families teach *me* and *them*.

When parents repeatedly miss soccer games, when driving kids to dance rehearsal is too much of a bother, when parents' schedules rule out time for family members being together, when night after night children are rushed off to bed—children learn an unmistakable truth: they are an inconvenience to their parents rather than a delight.

Covenant family gives children a future by giving them a history. Family is a context, a basis, a foundation for life. When family is unstable, broken or otherwise unsecured from the history of its covenant promises, all the members of the family suffer from insecurity. They feel a debilitating need to keep starting life over again—but they have been robbed of the covenant context for doing so. A lack of shared history leads to insecurity for the rest of our lives.

As we have seen, the first element of covenant—exchanging names—directly affects family. The same is true of the second element of covenant—sharing history. Our past shapes our future. But not just any aspect of our past has this powerful influence. Other than physical, bodily traumas or unusual psycho-emotional violation committed against us, the people with whom we are in covenant and the history we share with them impact our future the most.

Covenant can do two things for us. First, it helps us understand why things are as they are in our lives. We have made our own choices, and we must bear responsibility for our own sins. Not everything can be blamed on the power of covenant. But covenant violation by our parents or our spouse does account for many of the dysfunctions in our psyche.

Second, and more importantly, we can turn the power of covenant from destructive to constructive. We can become agents of good and blessing in the lives of our children and our spouse. By altering the way we act within covenant—becoming selfless and loving—we can alter the effect of covenant power in their future. Think of it as psycho-emotional genetic engineering, based on a fundamental spiritual law of the cosmos: what you sow you reap. Who I am today determines who the people with whom I am in covenant will be.

Never realising how fatalistic and discouraged we have become, we surrender a future God can still redeem for us. Shared history does shape our present experience. Tortured, dysfunctional family history creates the disorders in our soul. But within the covenant of family, God gives us a way to live today in the light of His history with us rather than according to our family history.

His covenant with us supersedes our family's covenant with us. By being obedient to God, we create a new shared history with our own family. Our obedience changes the future of our relationship with our spouse and with our children.

Dysfunctional families can be healed. How? By grabbing hold of the power of covenant and focusing on God's history with us—what He thinks about us; how He has shown himself faithful to us; what our identity is as new creations in Christ. Looking back with blame or bitterness hinders recovery. We have to face the fact that bad things have been done, but it will not help us to exchange blame for denial. Only by looking ahead and choosing to cling to God's relationship with us can we hope to live out a life-filled family future.

The power of family is the power of covenant. And that power can be tapped to transform your current family traumas into future family enjoyments.

6

For Better or for Worse

When Scotty started attending our singles group, he immediately affected everyone's mood. You couldn't be around this tall, athletic, mountain-climbing guy without feeling upbeat. His faith carried others with an optimism born of certainty rather than wishfulness.

Scotty's graphic arts business in a nearby town was booming, yet he maintained a balance of sharing his time and money with others. He was the perfect Christian yuppie—spiritual, successful, handsome and charming. Scotty's idea of a perfect day was hiking in Yosemite with Christian friends.

I watched Scotty fall in love.

Karen was a nursing student whose gentle, kind ways enthralled Scotty. Karen had a different sort of certainty about her than Scotty did. His was confidence. Hers was patience. Scotty overcame things. Karen came through them. Scotty could make you forget pain and press ahead. Karen helped you when pain wouldn't go away.

Not long after they announced their engagement, Scotty was hanging Christmas decorations at a church when the extension ladder he stood on gave way. He lunged for a beam, grasped it briefly enough for his legs to swing nearly parallel to the ground, then he plunged back-first to the floor.

In that moment, his world broke apart.

The medical realities were overwhelming: total paralysis from the chest down; partial use of one arm, slight use of the other; therapy and wheelchair for ever. His business closed. But his greatest torture had to do with Karen. He wanted to break off the engagement because he felt that the man who had promised himself to Karen was no longer able to keep his promise. He had offered her a whole body, financial security and a lifetime of hikes in Yosemite. That was the 'before' Scotty. The 'now' Scotty could offer her only an invalid's body, insurance settlements and a wheelchair to push. He felt that honour bid him release Karen from her promises since he could not keep his.

In thinking through all that had happened to him—the handicaps and hardships, the physical trauma and the emotional disappointment—Scotty had forgotten covenant. Karen never did. I'm sure she, too, had moments when she questioned why this had happened to the man she loved. Her life with him would never be the way she had imagined. That had to hurt.

But Karen knew that their disappointment was mutual. Through her tears one day, she asked me, 'Why would I turn away from the man I have said "yes" to when he needs me the most?' It wasn't pity that motivated her. It was covenant: for better or for worse; in sickness and in health . . .

Making Promises

A covenant creates a timeless world, insulated from the tyranny of changing circumstances. Of course, a covenant has no power to *control* life's circumstances—a lost job, a prolonged bout with cancer, the need to travel for one's job—but it can predetermine our responses towards one another in the midst of those circumstances.

How covenant does this can be found in the third and most obvious element of covenant: *promise making*. Stating promises outlines the nature and the boundaries of the covenant. After the covenant maker names the person with whom he or she wishes to covenant, and after the history of their relationship is rehearsed, promises of the covenant are made so that each will know what to expect from the other.

What a covenant outlines is up to the covenant maker, but the terms must be agreed to by all. When partners enter into covenant with each other, they voluntarily place themselves within the promised boundaries. And they pledge to remain there no matter what life may throw at them.

Thus, the promises act as benevolent restrictions, eliminating unsettling options. The promise to love does away with the prospect of not loving. Someone who stays within the covenant will not even entertain the idea of not loving. It gets rejected out of hand. Because of Karen's covenant promise—though she and Scotty were only engaged—it was inconceivable to her to walk away from him. As soon as Scotty recovered sufficiently, they were married. It was one of the most incredible weddings I have ever performed. Scotty and Karen's choice to remain true to covenant, true to each other, spoke a message to their wedding guests that echoes to this day.

Promise Making—God's Covenant

Karen's love for Scotty reminds me of God's promise to His people:

> I will betroth you to me *for ever*, I will betroth you in *righteousness* and *justice*, in *love* and *compassion*. I will betroth you in *faithfulness, and you will acknowledge the Lord* (Hos. 2:19–20, author's italics).

Forever means *concealed* or *vanished*. It connotes the vanishing point on a distant horizon—perpetual, always. Covenant has no time frame, no deadline. It has no expiration date, like perishable items in a store. It never gets used up. Time has no meaning within covenant because its promises remain the same today and for ever.

God uses powerful, spiritual forces to sustain this forever commitment of covenant with us. *Righteousness* is the foundation of God's rulership. It creates lasting quietness and settledness. People who live in righteousness—according to the way God intended them to live—have a peaceful habitation, and their dwelling places will be secured and undisturbed. Covenant and righteousness do not promise us life without challenges and regrets, but when we live in covenant with each other we face those traumas *together*, our relationship secured by promises to each other.

Since righteousness sustains covenant, the only power strong enough to break covenant is unrighteousness—sin. When we live with integrity, the Holy Spirit convicts us of wrong and directs us to acknowledge that wrong before it can destroy the covenant. A key promise of God's covenant is 'If we confess our sins, he is faithful and just and will forgive us our sins and purify us from all unrighteousness' (1 John 1:9). As we will learn later, the more that family members acknowledge their wrong attitudes and behaviours to one another, the stronger the family becomes.

By His covenant, God swears that He will never desert us or tire of us or refuse to draw us into His arms. He is faithful. His feelings for us never change. His love is constant and our standing with Him is never in question.

The *justice* God uses to betroth us to Himself is better translated *verdict*. In other words, God decides what is true and what is false. He judges to exonerate the innocent and to condemn the guilty. God does not take things at face value, but evaluates them with truth. God never makes rash decisions. He uses *justice* to maintain His covenant with us.

Likewise, *loving kindness* and *compassion* sustain covenant. No matter what we do, God is merciful to us. Little children make mistakes and do wrong things—they knock the porridge off the highchair tray, play with toy boats in the toilet and cry when they don't get their way. But loving parents never break off covenant with their children. It is the covenant maker, not the other party, who determines whether the covenant will be kept.

'I will betroth you to me in faithfulness.' *Faithfulness* implies fidelity, security, singleness of devotion. Literally, it means *firmness*, not a hardness but a steadiness. God remains faithful to what has been established. Being faithful means more than remaining loyal to a person. Biblically speaking, faithfulness is attached not to a *person* (our spouse), but to the *covenant* established with that person.

I am faithful to my vows, and that makes me faithful to my wife. God is faithful to His promise to me—to His own word. Since He cannot lie, He will never change His dealings with me even if I act differently from what I promised Him. That makes His covenant incredibly stable. It does not fluctuate according to foolish things that I do. It does not even consider my actions because it is based on His promises. This is the truest meaning of grace— undeserved favour and kindness towards us. It is created not by our works, but by His word.

Imagine the sheer power of God—unspoiled by self- interest, petty pride or insecurity, blind spots or wounding from childhood—to keep things right, to judge what is true and what isn't, to keep dealing with us out of kindness and compassion. Nothing that happens in the world can affect His dealings with us.

Paul described God's amazing covenant love like this:

> For I am convinced that neither death, nor life, nor angels, nor principalities, nor things present, nor things to come, nor powers, nor height, nor depth, nor any other created thing, shall be able to separate us from the love of God in Christ Jesus our Lord (Rom. 8:38–39 NASB).

Nothing can separate us from the covenant love of God— not tribulation, not distress; neither persecution nor peril nor violence. Nothing.

Hosea 2:19–20 ends with this promise: *Then you will know the Lord.* Casual relationships cannot offer us this kind of *knowing.* Full and complete disclosure between people comes only in covenant. God's commitment to us is ultimately a promise to reveal Himself to us. Again, covenant says, 'This is how things will always be between us,' and it ends up saying, 'This is who I really am. Through my constancy, you will come to know me. That is what I want in this relationship—to faithfully share my truest self with you through the years of our life together.'

The terms of a covenant are not conditional or variable. God fixes covenant relationship with us. Never again do we need to wonder whether God will forgive us or whether He is glad to have us come to Him. He will, and He is—always.

Christians who think God is angry with them or who feel they have done something too terrible for God to forgive do not understand covenant. Covenant says, 'This is how our relationship will *always be.*' Covenant eliminates uncertainty and ambiguity so that the people of the covenant can be absolutely secure in their standing with one another. The covenant secures the promises; the promises secure our standing with God, and that permanence allows us to be vulnerable enough to know God deeply. Without that assurance we would withhold ourselves from him. The relationship between God and the people of the covenant is no longer conditional; it is based, instead, on *covenant loyalty* and steadfast love.

Relationships surrounded by covenant have as much destructive, life-threatening stuff thrown at them as do non-covenant relationships. The difference is that the covering of covenant burns off and deflects much of what could hurt the relationship. 'No matter what' is the promise of covenant, and that promise nullifies most of the impact things might otherwise have.

Other than the Garden of Eden, the most obvious 'dwelling place' of covenant promise in the Old Testament is the Promised Land—the area of Canaan God said He would give His people. As God mapped out its borders and its provisions, it was clearly a place of great abundance and fulfilment. This geographic location is an analogy for what God has promised to us spiritually.

Over and over again we see the promises of God given to His people. Mostly they refer to what we will experience. He promises to take care of us, to provide for us, to lead us, to protect us, to see us safely through to the end. But covenants do have boundaries. As surely as they map out a *place* of abundance wherein we will be fulfilled and enriched beyond our wildest dreams, so too do they indicate a *place* beyond and outside those boundaries. Once He draws lines and borders, He separates the place of the covenant from those places outside it. Covenant is like sanctuary. Within covenant we are safe, and we can rest in the assurance of continued relationship. Outside covenant we are subjected to questions and uncertainty.

Promise Making—Marriage Covenant

Meaningful weddings include statements of promise spoken by the groom to the bride, and *vice versa*. 'For better or for worse, in sickness or in health . . . ' communicates tremendous security and rest. Contract marriages, conversely, imply, 'As long as you . . . I will . . . ' In a contract marriage, partners make sure the other fulfils his or her obligations before they fulfil their own. On the other hand, in a covenant marriage, we keep our promises *no matter what*.

Without covenant statements, a wife worries that if she gets sick, her husband may desert her; husbands fear that they will not make enough money to keep their wife happy. Failure and inadequacy torment the husband or the wife with what they will do to change the relationship.

To fully open ourselves to another, we must feel free from judgement or evaluation. If a husband senses that his performance—the way he handles the children or the bills—affects how his wife relates to him, he closes himself off from her. Likewise, a wife who feels that her standing with her husband depends on how she looks, how she performs in bed or how she compares with other women will not give her best to the relationship. The human soul was never made to live with those kinds of conditions and pressures.

Although we may settle for that kind of family because we do not know another way, we are actually craving covenant with one another. We want assurance that the questions of our relationship have all been answered *ahead of time.* If a wife communicates to her husband, 'I will always love you no matter how you do with the bills,' he will be free to respond to her offer of service, 'Can I help you in any way with the bills?' Just so, a wife who hears from her husband's heart, 'What you weigh has no bearing on how I feel about you' can then rest in his willingness to support her in her desire to lose weight.

Fear of rejection cripples a relationship. Covenant is a promise to never reject or forsake. Marriage is a covenant never to reject your spouse; a covenant always to seek the other's best.

Intimacy comes only after husband and wife feel secure that nothing they share with each other can jeopardise the relationship. Talking with a spouse about deeply personal issues—sharing the pain of past experiences, present worries or desires—is liberating. That's what marriage is for—not only to share a common history and a common future, but also to make our personal histories part of the common bond. In covenant family, it is safe to fully divest yourself and to be utterly open.

Pamela knows everything about me that I know. That makes me safe from everyone else. That also makes our relationship safe from the future because it is based on covenant, not on circumstance. On our wedding day we resolved to never again wonder or worry about where the future would take us or how it would challenge us because we knew that we would face that future together.

Like God's covenant with us, our covenant with our spouse can best be maintained with the forces of righteousness, justice, tenderness and faithfulness. If we choose to be the way God wants us to be; if we resolutely evaluate what is happening to our family from within and without; if we act kindly towards each other, and remember the covenant we have within, it is less likely that our families will fail. Our spouses may choose another way in a determined effort to break their vows, but if we are vigilant to confess unrighteousness, then living God's righteous way of life will maintain covenant sanctity for our family.

Problems come when Dad runs his family on the basis of a few Scriptures on submission, while neglecting the heart of compassion and the fruit of the Spirit. Covenant safety falters when Mum controls everyone and everything in her angry, frustrated need to justify herself. When husbands and wives judge each other and introduce into the relationship condemnation, shame and rejection, they sacrifice the pure power of God's justice. Our resentment grows because 'he didn't take out the rubbish in time' or 'she spends so much time and money clothes shopping, it's a wonder we ever eat.' Before long, kindness and mercy give way to unforgiveness. And covenant suffers.

If marriage is only the sum of our experiences together, then the balance is always in question. Every marriage has seasons. Without the permanence of covenant and those forces that maintain it, family is endangered. Family is supposed to be a place of promise—like God's Promised Land. How could the people of God live securely if He told them that their boundaries would fluctuate with the seasons? Or if He told them their food supply would vary from year to year?

Such would not be the Promised Land, but the uncertain land.

Promise Making—Family Covenant

At the heart of a functional family is stability and longevity. I can remember Pamela's exclamation not long after Hilary was born: 'I will be her mother for the rest of my life.' Nothing can change the biological, medical reality of motherhood. And nothing is supposed to alter the spiritual, psycho-emotional covenant of parenthood.

It is no accident that we speak of *having* children when they are born. Kids belong. They belong with family, to parents—not in some distorted notion of being owned or used any way the parents desire, but belonging in the sense of having a place for which they were made.

Think of it this way—children are made to fit perfectly in family. When children do not fit, when they seem to be the odd one out or when they feel they do not belong, that is a sure sign of a dysfunctional family. Most children go through a stage when they imagine that they are adopted. That is normal in their junior school years. But families with 'black sheep' are dysfunctional in some way—usually it means significant promises made to that family member were broken. Jilted children deal with their disappointments by becoming 'odd'. 'Not fitting in' becomes part of their identity; they are forced to exchange their family heritage for a surrogate parentage.

Parents often tell me they make private promises to their unborn child. They promise what they will do in the years ahead with the baby as she or he grows up—everything from flying kites to going on long walks to talking about life. We promise our womb-children that we will be there for them, coach their soccer team, take them camping and push them on the swing at the park.

Even before we meet our children, we write a hundred promissory notes to them, and we indebt ourselves to them for the rest of our lives.

What we solemnly vow to them is that we will be the best parents to them that the world has ever seen. The promises give expression to—and may even create—the deep bonding we feel with these little people whom we have not yet met.

My point is not to dredge up guilt for those of us who have not fulfilled all the idealised promises we made to our first born (the realities of each successive child tend to reduce the fervour of such promises). Instinctively, we know to make promises—promises we never even think to make with anyone else's children. Their kids may be better looking and better behaved, but we instinctively promise to be the best mum or dad *only* to children who belong to us in our family covenant—whether they are born into it or adopted.

I advise single parents to look for these unspoken promises to their young children by any person the single parent seriously considers marrying. Only a spouse who instinctively makes promises to the entire family can become more than a resented interloper.

True family is an atmosphere of promise. At its basic level, covenant family promises shelter, food and clothing. It says it will take care of the member's needs. Family isn't just a place to crash and eat. Any place can be that. Family is the promise that you are always welcome to sleep and eat here—there will always be a place for you.

True family promises belonging and acceptance for a lifetime. By offering children roots, it offers them a secure identity no matter what the future holds. Real family promises to see the real you and to love the real you. Functional family makes and carries out its promises to family members. Though promises are inadvertently broken in the hectic pace of family life, perpetual fulfilment rather than disappointment marks the promises made to one another.

Parenting is essentially the task of teaching children

about life. So family promises an extended tutorial on the subject—everything from hot ovens and look-both-ways street crossings to hair doing and finger snapping. Children intuitively respond to promises. Promises are personal and powerful. They are the essence of covenant. The more promises made and kept in a family, the more powerfully family can secure children's future.

Promise Making—Dysfunctional Family

We now approach an area that is painful and disappointing for many adults. Most of us have difficult memories of broken promises in our childhood. Some readers may already have traced their personal dysfunctions to the covenant violation of broken promises; other readers will begin to realise that their childhood was so bitter and bent because family covenant never existed for them. And for some, the promises actually were curses.

Allen

Allen had been affected by the power of family—only he didn't realise it. He was told so often by his parents that he didn't do things right (like his older brother did), he began to believe it.

In fact, he could only recall a time or two when he actually heard those biting, critical words from his parents. But his parents' subtle indictment of his abilities—and ultimately, his personhood—rattled around in his soul for years. Without realising it, his parents' contrasting treatments of Allen and his older brother condemned him for life.

The unconscious sentence imposed on Allen by the family tribunal was: 'You can never legitimately relax with your wife and kids. You must always feel guilty for not working. Since your work is not good enough, not acceptable, your only redemption will be to work longer and more. Just as you know you are unaccepted in this family in which you have grown up, so you will always doubt that your future family members sincerely enjoy you.'

Until Allen understood the incredible power of family and covenant, he could not explain to himself, much less to his wife and children, why he was so driven. He felt uncomfortable unless he was working. He learned that from his parents' perverse promise about him. What his parents had the power to do—settle and secure his thoughts about his validity as a person—they unintentionally squandered, and they indebted him to a cruel, unforgiving self-image.

The only difference between promises and curses is the kind of future they spell out for people. Both promises and curses say 'This is what will happen.' In the covenant model we are examining in this book, we see that promises made in a family become curses when they are broken. Allen was cursed by his family. His parents broke their covenant promises to him.

Allen is learning to break that curse by keeping his own covenantal promises to his wife and children. As long as he focuses on what the Bible tells him about God's verdict on his life, Allen can resist responding to the way he was raised. This is no easy process. Too bad Allen has had to expend so much energy repairing what was so thoughtlessly broken in his family upbringing.

The only lasting recovery begins with *forgiveness*. As you remember disappointments and unfulfilled expectations, use them as beginning points of forgiveness and reconciliation. Any grudge you hold against others will work against you.

Adult Children of No Promises

As I mentioned, a dysfunctional family never carries through on its promise of belonging for children. The children feel like unwanted intruders—maybe they are ignored and treated with indifference, or maybe they have been told by parents, 'We never wanted you anyway.'

'Can't you do anything right?' sends unmistakable and devastating signals to a child that he or she does not fit in this family place. Dysfunctional families communicate alienation instead of acceptance; independence instead of interconnection. Additionally, if children suspect that parents provide food, shelter and other necessities only because they *have to*, not because they *want to*, those children feel guilty, confused and ashamed. Later, those torturous feelings can turn into rebellion and indifference.

Youngsters who are unwanted or who never receive promises will look for a surrogate family whose members will provide for them. This explains the phenomenal attraction of youth gangs. Gangs are based on covenant principles; that is why they exert such powerful influence in the lives of the members. Gangs become the covenant family the members were denied at home. Gangs make and keep promises; members are loyal to each other. Gangs have initiations to define the boundaries of their covenant—once you are in, you are accepted, protected and provided for. Conversely, what is asked of you, you do.

Children who receive no promises from their family, no assurances about the future, intuitively slip into a survival mode. They lose interest in their own future—choosing the pleasure of the moment above planning for the future. A dysfunctional family that does not promise what it should eats away at a child's self-worth.

The children determine that they aren't worth the time

or the trouble of meaningful promises made and kept by parents. With nothing much to look forward to in their family, they presume they cannot expect much from life.

Low motivation to better ourselves through education, hard work or sacrifice can be traced back to voided promises from our family. Rather than laziness or indifference, our behaviour mirrors the lack of expectation and hope modelled for us in childhood.

When parents don't care what time children come home at night, or refuse to do simple things like helping them with homework, the children pick up definite signals about how unimportant, how unpromising they are. And we treat ourselves the way our family treated us.

Adult Children of Promise Breakers

As tragic as a family that offers no promises is the family that breaks its promises. Perhaps out of convenience, these parents promise a future to the children to keep from having to do anything now. 'Someday', 'Maybe tomorrow', 'When things slow down at the office'—these are the tags on little-promises-to-be-broken. Some of them are unavoidable, but when they become habitual, that indicates dysfunction.

So promises go unfulfilled. And increasingly confused children learn to disbelieve those people they instinctively should believe. Once children learn not to trust their parents, they learn not to trust anyone. They come to rely on themselves alone—leading to a life of emotional isolation.

Do your children seldom pay attention to what you say? You would do well to rehearse your record of promises kept and broken. Promises become little more than ways of putting children off, and the put-offs eventually establish a pattern for the children to repeat with their spouse and children.

Adult Children of Promise Extractors

Dysfunctional families violate the promise element of covenant. But there is even more to it than promises not made and promises not kept. *Who* makes the promises—and what kind of promises they are—also distinguishes true family from dysfunctional family.

In true family, parents are promise makers because they are the covenant makers. Real covenant is a secure promise of care by the stronger and more able to the weaker and less able. Parents establish covenant with children by giving them names, by establishing a history of loving and care, and by making promises.

When a child is forced to make promises to a parent, God's intended order for family is disrupted. These promises are usually extracted for the convenience of the parent or to cover up wrong behaviour. For example, parents in a dysfunctional home might make a child promise never to tell that Daddy touched them on their privates, or that Mummy was kissing Daddy's best friend. Or, children might be sworn to pretence—not to tell anyone how little money the family has, always appearing religiously correct in public (especially at church), or never using the same swear words Dad uses.

Certainly, some promises parents ask children to make are harmless. Parents going out to dinner may ask the children to promise to behave; a parent may ask a child to promise to clean her room when she comes home from school. These promises shape and reinforce desired behaviour; they are not heavy burdens placed on the consciences of little people. Parents should take care not to make even these little promises too frequent or too weighty.

Forcing children to provide for, to take care of, or to make a place for the parents, results in emotional panic.

When the burden of the covenant falls to the children, they sense the danger they are in—the danger of a conditional contract. The implied threat is that if the children do not keep their promises to the parent, the parent will end the relationship.

This reversal of roles is dysfunctional. Adults who grew up in such homes can be called *adult children of promise extractors.* They tend to be irresponsible, avoidance types, or compulsive worriers who over-plan for every imaginable contingency.

Finally, keeping the distorted promises of a dysfunctional family almost always violates integrity or identity. Asked to do something they know isn't right, promise makers must deny themselves to keep their word. Contrast that with what promises were meant to be: part and parcel of personhood.

Family was meant to give its members a promising future by making and keeping promises about that future. Providing a secure future for our children is equally as important as giving them the necessities of life, arranging for a good education and teaching them good life habits.

If covenant promises are broken, no substitute promises, no surrogate bonding will repair the damage. But if they are kept, they have the power to secure family members with one another and with the people they meet throughout their lives. Promise keeping creates optimistic children and hopeful spouses. We can make or break promises; the choice belongs to us. What we do will either make or break our family. That is the power of covenant.

7

In the Sight of God

Power tends to corrupt, and absolute power corrupts absolutely. Sir J. Dalberg's often quoted maxim is not so much an indictment against power itself as it is against the heart of people bent on evil. Unfortunately, human beings usually succumb to power's temptation.

Although power is a neutral force, it can be used for evil. For instance, the power of the printing press gave common people access to the Bible, but it also provided political propagandists with a tool for exploiting those same people. It could print truth or lies. Likewise, atomic energy can power cities or destroy them. Neutral forces can be beneficial or harmful, depending on the user's motives.

Electricity, natural gas and even the rays of the sun can be blessing or curse. We take these powers for granted until something goes wrong. We forget their force because we are so accustomed to their blessings. That is how it is with family and covenant—the shorted wires, broken pipes or unwise exposures to the sun can lead to problems. Even basic tools of family can be dangerous if mishandled.

While Pamela and I were college students, I offered to help her cut some mat boards for a design class she was taking. It wasn't long before we had a good system going—she pencilled lines on the mats; I set the metal ruler on those lines, and with repeated pulls on the Stanley knife, I cut through the mats. To keep the knife from cutting its own crooked path across the mat, I butted it against the metal ruler, held firmly on the surface of the mat by my thumb and forefinger. Well, you may have guessed it . . . the blade jumped above the ruler's edge and sliced evenly into my thumb.

Sharp knives cut. That's their purpose and their power.

The knife that allowed me to help Pamela with her assignment was the same blade that cut and scarred my thumb. The only distinction between good and harm was the direction the blade went. Anyone could have predicted what would happen to me because I was cutting the mats unwisely.

Power can be misused—either intentionally or unintentionally.

Judging Consequences

In a world of good and evil, of right and wrong, consequences can be good or bad. From the moment Adam and Eve broke covenant with God, they faced the consequences of that act. Prior to eating the forbidden fruit, they knew nothing of judgement—discerning between good and evil. Adam and Eve did not realise their disobedience would cause things to turn out so differently from how God intended them to be. They did not know what dire consequences they would ultimately introduce into the world through their disobedience.

Satan tempted Adam and Eve to disobey, first, by telling them that what God said was not true, and second, by telling them the consequences would be good, not bad. He lied about God's motives and judgement. The good and bountiful world Adam and Eve lived in didn't just happen.

It existed because God judged that's the way things should be. When Adam and Eve chose a different way, they altered the world from the one God originally designed.

I used poor judgement when I cut Pamela's mat boards. I didn't think through what would happen. Though not on a par with the fall of humankind, my nearly severed thumb resulted, like the fall, from faulty judgement.

Consequence is part of judgement. That is why *judging consequences* is the essence of good judgement. When parents discipline their children, they try to teach them about consequences. A car engine that freezes up because it has no oil, friends who are hurt because we forgot their birthdays, a wife who grows distant because her husband shows her no attention—these are consequences.

Action and reaction. Cause and effect. The world as we know it is bound in consequences.

God, the first covenant maker, was also the first consequence maker. Every covenant has consequences because every covenant is a force. It can add significant blessing and good to your relationships, but if not used properly, it can also introduce trauma.

As we have seen, the law of gravity keeps order and makes things easier than they would otherwise be. The arduous repair job astronauts did in space on the Hubble telescope would have been relatively simple if done on earth. Weightlessness made the job difficult.

Gravity is good—unless we ignore or violate its effects. Because gravity shapes our world, sensible people do not disregard it. The power that keeps our feet on the ground is the same force that breaks a vase knocked from a table. Gravity has consequences. So does covenant. Covenant can keep our feet on the ground, or it can break us.

Accepting Consequences

We come now to the fourth and final element of covenant —*accepting consequences*. Covenant carries with it an automatic evaluation of how well promises are kept. Covenant automatically releases into the lives of the covenant parties consequences for keeping or not keeping their vows. Judgement is built into covenant.

That makes covenant risky. But its risks are different from the risks of contract relationship. In a contract relationship, I guard myself from the consequences of someone else's behaviour. I protect myself and my interests from their actions. I hedge myself in with conditions and stipulations. In a dispute, the battle lines are clear: me against them; if they win, I lose; if I win, they lose. Contracts are essentially contests between people. Judges decide between the parties, in favour of one and against the other.

But with covenant, the judgement is altogether different. God joins husband and wife with unconditional, covenantal promises. Consequently, God does not judge in favour of one party or the other. Instead, He judges the integrity of the covenant—whether it has been kept or broken. The judgement in covenant is not *between* the covenant parties. Since both husband and wife are in the covenant *together*, they will *both* be affected by the consequences of blessing or of curses. Covenant is win/win or lose/lose.

I'm not saying that God doesn't care which of the two violated covenant. Rather, that judgement is about another matter other than covenant. God warns us not to cause *anyone* to stumble. Acceptable behaviour is outlined throughout the New Testament. For instance, if we cause a 'little one to stumble,' our judgement will be severe. 'God will judge the adulterer and all the sexually immoral'

(Heb. 13:4), but that same judgement also falls on 'whatever else is contrary to the sound doctrine' (1 Tim. 1:10). Our sins against others come under God's judgment against *all* unrighteousness. The wages of sin—any kind of sin—is death.

All sin violates covenant with God, and those who sin suffer the consequences. Violations against our family covenant create additional consequences for our lives.

Covenant consequence is one force; grace and mercy from God are other forces. God comforts the afflicted. Victims receive mercy and solace from Him. God offers strength, counsel, help and recovery to everyone who has been traumatised by others' sins. His judgement is always on behalf of the oppressed and downtrodden. This judgement applies to everyone, all the time; it is no more or less active in covenant situations than in relationships outside of covenant.

So when I say that covenant judgement introduces consequences to both members of the covenant, I am not implying that the violator 'gets off as lightly' as the violated. In fact, it usually seems that the violated ends up 'paying more' than do the ones who break covenant. The hardness of heart of the violator only makes it seem that way. In reality, both covenant parties suffer the same consequence spiritually. Because of God's covenant to restore us, there is grace and comfort available to the violated.

Perhaps it would be more helpful to say that the family covenant itself is judged. An unbroken covenant releases untold blessing; the judgement of a broken covenant unleashes untold destruction. Think of covenant as a rushing river that can power turbines or devastate buildings in its flood path. The water and the power are the same, but the results depend on how they are channelled.

So it is with covenant. If it is kept according to its promises, covenant can be transformed into an incredibly beneficial resource. If it does not follow its proper course, it can destroy the homes it would have empowered.

Witness Calling

In the wedding ceremony itself, this aspect of covenant—accepting consequences—is manifested by the calling of witnesses. Though witness calling is involved in any process of judgement—a trial or an investigation—we often miss its significance at a wedding. Usually at the beginning of the formal wedding ceremony, the pastor will say, 'We are gathered together in the sight of God and these witnesses . . .'

After declaring his name, history and promises, a true covenant maker calls for someone to act as a witness to what has been promised. The witnesses at a wedding become living reminders to the covenant maker that he has bound himself not only to his wife, but also to his promises to her. The wife binds herself similarly by her promises in the presence of God and the witnesses.

Covenant makers must demonstrate an understanding of covenant. This is not a contract to be witnessed so that we can enforce its contents on the other party; this is a covenant. It has potential for advantage, security and blessing, or for disadvantage, insecurity and curse. Covenant comes with a manufacturer's warning on its label. Covenant consequences go beyond judgement of how husband and wife treat each other. Covenant consequences also extend to whether promises to each other are kept.

Accepting Consequences—God's Covenant

God made covenants with an exact pattern to them.

Without calling for a witness and a judge, God could not offer us a true covenant. Promises alone are one thing; covenants are another. Parties of a covenant willingly acknowledge their accountability to the promises. They must give account to one greater than themselves for how they live out the covenant.

God's covenant with us is unique because God swears by Himself to uphold His words. He acts as His own witness and judge because there is none greater than the Lord.

Because of this, we can begin to understand the significance of God's faithfulness to His word. If God broke His promise, it would unleash destruction that would destroy the cosmos. His word made the worlds and maintains them. It is eternal.

That explains eternal life in heaven. In heaven, God's word is not contradicted or lied about. It will not be violated; there will be no sin. These things will last for ever: God's word, the place made by that word, and those of us who 'have been born again, not of perishable seed, but of imperishable, through the living and enduring word of God' (1 Pet. 1:23).

That is covenant: the same promises, the same place, the same people—for ever.

God's covenant with us—like all true covenants—invokes both a blessing and a curse. That is why God says to us, 'See, I am setting before you today a blessing and a curse . . . the blessing if you obey . . . the curse if you disobey' (Deut. 11:26–28). The choice to live within covenant is always ours, but the consequences of the choice are fixed within the covenant itself. We cannot separate covenant promises from covenant consequences. The blessing, or the curse, is not added as an afterthought to the covenant. It is an inseparable part of the promises.

People who wonder why God would send people to hell do not understand the nature of covenant. Covenant has consequences. Heaven or hell. Life or death. Blessing or curse. Covenant creates a spiritual cause-and-effect relationship. When the terms of the covenant are followed, the covenant produces blessing. If they are violated, it unleashes horrible consequences in the lives of the people it was meant to bless. Humanity violated previous covenants with God, so He established one final covenant with eternal consequences.

God's offer of covenant relationship through Jesus Christ restores lost relationship with Him and gives us true life. The *eternal* life of the covenant not only lasts longer than normal life, but it also has another dimension. God's covenant offers us joy, well-being, health, peace, security, satisfaction, meaning and relationship with Him. His covenant with us—which He established by sending His Word (Jesus Christ) to us as a promise—has one intent. God wants to secure and to save lost people.

Anything powerful enough to restore our violated relationship with God, and to rescue us from our own sin, is too powerful to be ignored without eternal consequences. The power to forgive is the same power to condemn.

Accepting Consequences—Marriage Covenant

Those who question the value of a public wedding ceremony do not understand the necessity of witness calling as part of covenant. A wedding is a public invitation to friends and family to hold the couple to their covenant vows. The couple might ignore our reminders, but we have the right to tell them when they are behaving inconsistently with their promise.

Family as covenant takes on awesome proportions

when viewed in the light of witness calling and consequential invocation of judgement. Covenants are not neutral and they are not to be toyed with or treated lightly.

No wonder marriage—a source of emotional, mental and physical fulfilment—can create indescribable agonies. How many people have been broken by the breaking of marriage covenant? Divorce is so damaging because it violates the promise statements of the covenant. Instead of covering the fragile inner self, divorce exposes and rejects it. The pain can take years to get over.

We must understand covenant as a spiritual force—able to bring bounty and abundance, or poverty and loss. The spiritual consequences cannot be overlooked. We cannot recover from a violated covenant with a former spouse by being bitter, hateful and unforgiving. Such attitudes, no matter how understandable and legitimate in the eyes of the world, deny us the provisions of recovery promised in God's covenant.

Divorce is so common these days that it is accepted as one of the hazards of marriage. To young couples, many of whom come from broken homes, the trauma of divorce seems normal and almost unavoidable. But entertaining the possibility that husband and wife will not stay together the rest of their lives works against family as it should be. In families where divorce is contemplated (much less accomplished) the result is hugely disruptive for all the family members.

God does not punish innocent victims of divorce by ripping apart their hearts and souls. Rather, having positioned themselves as parties to a covenant, victims of divorce have inescapably linked themselves to the outcome of that covenant—either for triumph or for trauma.

Casual marriage does not carry casual consequences.

No matter how the covenant of marriage is entered into by a woman and a man, the subsequent blessings from keeping the oaths, or the curses from violating those oaths, are powerful beyond understanding.

Within the covenant itself are the seeds of either bountiful or blighted harvest. The judge does not arbitrarily impose dire consequences on people of failed covenants. The covenants themselves do. We can see, then, why marriage should be considered carefully, and entered into only with someone who has a history of faithfulness and evidence of desire to nurture us.

The blessings of the marriage covenant explain why God so often uses marriage as an analogy to express the nature of His relationship to us. What peace there is in knowing Pamela will love me and stay with me until death. On our wedding day, when I was driving to the church with my best man, Michael, I remember thinking, *Well, that's that. I will never again have to wonder who I should date, how a woman feels towards me or who I should love. It's all settled.* So much uncertainty leaves us when we covenant for life with our spouse.

I am joined with Pamela, and she with me—always. Forsaking all other people, emotions, circumstances and encumbrances, we will stick to and by each other. Knowing that Pamela will always love me gives me great peace. And resolving to love only her gives me singleness of heart and direction. For both of us, that determined and lifelong devotion shelters us from the confusing onslaught of options for other intimacies.

Accepting Consequences—Family Covenant
Family is a covenant parents make with their children. God meant this covenant to secure maximum blessing for

children. Family shapes the way children think about themselves, the way they view the world and the way they feel towards other people. For the most part, children turn out the way they are raised, but much of the raising is done without parents even being conscious of what they are doing for their children.

What children experience in their family upbringing will affect them for ever, unless God miraculously reshapes their psyche. It is the only world they know initially, and their parents are their champions, their heroes. Family shapes their future by how it treats them. Within true family covenant, parents accept the charge of carrying out certain responsibilities towards their children.

The Bible expresses these duties in several different ways. Here are five elements that parents should promise to give to the children of their covenant:

1. Affection. Love them not only in your heart, but also with your smiles, your hugs, your tender words and your gentle ways. God cherishes us, as a mother tenderly caresses her newborn. We are to do the same with our children.

2. Attention. Keep your eye on them not only for their safety, but also when they perform their silly dramas in the living room, when they are trying something new and when they play in a ball game. God's eyes are ever on us, and He watches over us without sleeping. His thoughts towards us are more than the sands of the sea.

3. Instruction. Fill them with the benefit of learning and experiences from your life, so that they do not have to learn the hard way. God is good and upright, so He teaches us how to live. Jesus offers His yoke and His instruction to us. We are called to do the same for our children.

4. Promotion. Encourage them by demonstrating your confidence that they are wonderful and that they will be successful in God's plan for their lives. Just as God believes in us, so too should we give our children a knowing nod, encouraging smile, or promising wink that says, 'You can do it.'

5. Protection. Keep them safe, not only from physical harm but also from exposure to attitudes, experiences and thoughts that might traumatise their souls or jeopardise their spiritual well-being. God watches over us and delivers us from evil. We are privileged to do the same for our children.

Just because parents are Christians and faithfully attend church does not mean they are faithfully nurturing their children. Being a believer in Jesus and being the parent of Jenny are not the same thing. Perhaps that is why most churches have separate ceremonies to dedicate a child and to mark an adult's conversion or confirmation. Whether in an infant dedication before the congregation, or as part of the promises made in public during infant baptism, Christian parents through the ages have recognised the need to call witnesses to the promises they make in covenant with their children.

When we cry out against the dysfunctional family, and look to our family upbringing for answers to our present psycho-emotional disorders, we unknowingly acknowledge the consequence of covenant: 'I am the way I am because of what happened to me in my family. My parents were not affectionate. My mum yelled a lot. My brothers teased me unmercifully. My uncle abused me.'

These are cries for justice. They are pleas for judgement. They are echoes of broken covenant.

Continual threats and rage towards us traumatise us.

But when they come from our mother, the damage is worse. Likewise, petty, critical and perfectionistic expectations exhaust and discourage us. But when it is our father, the discouragement strikes deeper into our soul.

People with whom I have no meaningful relationship do not normally affect my inner soul for good or ill. If I have no bonding with someone, the person cannot get at the inner part of me. This is because of covenant. Only when I have established some measure of covenant with a friend or family member do I become vulnerable to him or her.

Accepting Consequences—Dysfunctional Family

People do not subsist alone. Psychologists have long suspected that many personality disorders begin in childhood, and most such disorders are a consequence of distortions in relationship with other individuals. Only in the past forty years or so has serious attention been given to family as a whole system or culture adversely impacting individuals.

Families are cultures, each differing from one another in their customs, patterns, subtleties, manners and expectations. You might say families have a life of their own, beyond the individual lives of their members. American culture is different from Dutch culture, and within the American culture, what goes in California is different from what is acceptable in Virginia; and Santa Cruz has a different lifestyle from that of Los Angeles.

Likewise, families have nuances of expected reactions, ways to talk about or avoid unpleasantries and when and how to show affection.

Although often unspoken, the cultural trappings of family are strongly ingrained by everything from benign reinforcement to violent threats. For example, a family may expect that all members get advanced degrees in college. Although such pressure may never be verbalised, it is still there. The child who does not live up to the expectation becomes a cultural outcast—possibly without any of the individual family members realising it. Even though lip service might be paid to 'everyone doing what they want to do after high school,' the cultural expectations of the family system are communicated more convincingly.

Children of this family who do not go to college become enigmas even to themselves and will most likely feel ambivalent about any vocational pursuit. No matter how distorted the system itself may be, failing or refusing to conform to the system always disorientates the family members. Though sometimes perverse, family is reality, especially to children.

Dysfunctional family systems go beyond expectations about college. Addictive family systems, for instance, exert overwhelming cultural pressure on family members to live out unspoken expectations and to live under certain rules that can rob children of their sanity.

In some family cultures, Dad is allowed to express frustration or anger vehemently and violently. He can scream, hit, throw things, break doors, curse and storm. Everyone in these families knows that such outbursts are his privilege alone. Family becomes the place where Dad can act any way he wants. Dad is the signal giver, and woe to the family member who misses or misinterprets his signals. Or even worse, there are no consistent signals by which a child can navigate. Quickly, Mum and kids learn that the only allowable response is passive silence. Anything else meets with an even worse fate.

'That's just the way Dad is' covers up children's confusion about what is wrong, teaching them unspoken rules of life. In this family, a child learns one or several of these 'truths' about life:

1. *One day the privilege of unrepented, unacknowledged anger will be mine.*
2. *An important mark of authority is the privilege to live outside the rules under which others live.*
3. *It is normal to live under abusive, threatening conditions.*
4. *It is never safe to be around Dad or other male authority figures.*

Destructive though the father's behaviour is in this case, the real damage done to the child comes from a family system that tolerates and (even worse) considers such activity normal. In other words, if the family culture taught the child that Dad is wrong to fly into a rage, the effects of Dad's temper would be much less severe in the child's life.

If Dad had to deny himself, repent of his aberrant behaviour and ask the family's forgiveness, the child would learn different lessons about life and how it works. The child would still feel the temporary sting of the anger, but no lasting psychological damage would be done if everyone agreed that Dad was wrong.

A healthy family is not a place where everyone is perfectly behaved all the time. It isn't always as placid as *Leave it to Beaver* leads us to believe. A good, healthy family can absorb the effects of lost tempers because such outbursts are clearly identified as wrong. They are forgiven, not just tolerated or ignored. They are the exception rather than the rule.

The breakdown of covenant threatens children. When family covenant dissolves, a child's whole world is shattered—and with it the sense of what is right, a sense of continuity and roots, and understanding of themselves. Nothing is as it was. No matter what the issues between Mum and Dad, a child interprets divorce as abandonment and covenant breaking. Failing to provide emotional or physical security, abandoning or otherwise breaking promise with children disturbs their emotional equilibrium for years to come.

Unkind, accusing words spoken by a parent or by a sibling can follow a child through adulthood. The taunts of an older brother about his sister's appearance can sentence her to a lifetime of feeling ugly. Children whose opinions are never recognised become adults who doubt themselves and fear making decisions.

A child who hears 'You'll never amount to anything' can become a workaholic adult. 'Can't you ever do anything right?' can doom children to fail again and again as they grow up, or it can teach them that their self-worth is tied to success. If Mum is unforgiving and hateful towards men, daughters can grow up to have warped views of intimacy with the opposite sex.

Neglectful dads beget bewildered sons who may crave male approval and affection, and who may be tempted to gain that affection sexually. Rejection by his father can lead a son to the unnatural desire of sexual intimacy with men. Families that do not show physical affection may produce children either too curious about physical touching— leading to promiscuity—or too self-conscious about it— producing an inability to be affectionate with their loved ones.

Why do children become the kinds of adults they do? The answer goes beyond the fact that they are impressionable and easily damaged when they are young. That is true, of course, but they are so vulnerable within their families because God constructed family to work that way.

Family is a promise to parents who desperately love their kids. The promise is the promise of covenant: what your children become is not a consequence of luck and circumstances beyond your control. Their future can be secured, to a large extent, by your determination to maintain covenant with them. We parents too easily dismiss the power inherent in family to protect our children.

True family can look forward with confidence to its children's futures. As powerful as is the destruction from dysfunctional families, so is the construction in the lives of people raised in true family. The syndrome suffered by adult children of substance-addicted parents is less powerful than the syndrome to be enjoyed by adult children of family-covenanted parents.

The covenant comes with a curse, but family was meant to bless. And it can bless you even if you have already suffered some of the curse. Simply put, the incredible wreckage we see around us stemming from dysfunctional families is hopeful proof that *family*—the real *family* intended by God—can do far more in people's lives than most of us imagine.

Put in the light of my experience with the Stanley knife, covenant can be seen as a sharp knife meant to enhance the design and development of our children. Covenant is an essential tool.

The knife can cut crooked or straight. How the knife is used, whether or not it cuts along an established boundary, how much firmness and attention it is given—all these determine where the blade is headed. To this day I have a healthy respect for Stanley knives. I remember how easily one sliced my thumb. I know how sharp they are. And that makes me careful whenever I pick one up. But it also helps me appreciate what they can do.

Covenant is capable of incredible cuts, too.

8

Covenant:
A Chance to be Deeply
Known

Having examined the nature of covenant, we're left with the question: how does living in covenant translate into everyday life? There are several vital areas where covenant affects us all. See if you can identify one of these areas in the scenarios below:

Scene one: Alison and Tyler go to their pastor in a last-ditch effort to salvage their marriage. As Alison sits listening to the pastor, tears quietly slip down her cheeks. Finally, she says, 'Tyler doesn't know me any more. He has no idea who I really am or what I need to be happy. And I don't think he wants to—he's let everything slide for too long. It's too late now.'

Tyler interrupts, 'Well it cuts both ways, you know. When was the last time you did something I wanted to do? You don't seem to have much time for me either.'

Scene two: Rayna is a fifteen-year-old who had her hair cut in a style she knew her mother didn't approve of. When her mother first saw it, she grounded Rayna for a month. In retaliation, Rayna yelled back, 'You don't care about what I want to do. You only care about what it looks like to your friends at church. You aren't interested in me. You won't let me be myself, you want to control me. You don't have a clue about who I am.' With that, Rayna rushed out of the house, slamming the door behind her.

Scene three: Alex stood on the bridge and looked down at the cool deep water. He imagined how easy it would be to sink beneath its smooth surface. *Why should I go on? he asked himself. Who really cares if I live or die? The people at work would wonder why I did it, and some family would miss me. But who really knows me? My counsellor does a little. But she's paid to listen, it's her job. If she wasn't paid, she wouldn't care either. Nobody would.* Slowly, Alex climbed over the bridge railing and prepared to jump into the swirling waters below.

These scenes are imaginary, but they ring true. Why? Because, at some point we all ask ourselves, *Does anyone want to know me—I mean really know me?* If the answer is no, it plunges us into gnawing despair. What is so important about being deeply known by another person? Why do we yearn so for disclosure and intimacy with another human being?

The answer can be found in God's grand scheme for making people in the first place. God wanted to share Himself—all that He is, all that He had—because that is the nature of love. God is love (1 John 4:8), and that love sought an object upon which to lavish itself. God's longing to love moved Him to create us so that He could love us. We were made in love and we were made to be loved.

The First Love Story

Remember the story of Adam and Eve? As soon as Adam was fashioned out of the dust, he viewed the entire catalogue of created beings, identifying and naming each species of bird and animal. But when he finished, he still felt empty. Why? What was he looking for? A suitable companion—someone with whom he could share his life.

God recognised that need and fashioned Eve out of Adam's side, making her bone of Adam's bone, flesh of his flesh. The instant Adam saw Eve, he knew she was what he was looking for. Unlike the animals, Eve resembled Adam, and that similarity of body and soul made possible a love for each other.

In the same way, all people are made in God's image. No other beings are created with His likeness. The angels and cherubim are beautiful and majestic, but they do not bear the spiritual *image* of God. He does not love them the way He loves us. God gave the life of His Son to save people from their sins; God did not offer His Son to redeem fallen angels. God loves those beings who bear His likeness. Likewise, Adam loved the woman taken from His side, the one who bore His likeness.

Created in God's image, we share certain characteristics with Him. We want to love as God loves. Love longs for oneness and deep communion with another. Love compels us to secure lasting relationships. Love is highly motivated. It seeks to know and be known. It wants intimacy. It offers disclosure.

God knows everything there is to know about us. David, a king of Israel, was so struck by God's knowing him, he wrote a song about it:

O Lord, you have searched me and you know me.
You know when I sit and when I rise; you perceive

my thoughts from afar. You discern my going out and my lying down; you are familiar with all my ways. Before a word is on my tongue you know it completely, O Lord. You hem me in—behind and before; you have laid your hand upon me. Such knowledge is too wonderful for me, too lofty for me to attain (Ps. 139:1).

Not only does God know us completely, but He also wants to be known by us. That is why when the trumpet sounds 'we will know as we have been known'. It's all part of God's eternal plan of love. The letter to the Hebrews gives us a glimpse of God's heart. He wants 'knowing' to be a two-way thing.

This is the covenant I will make with the house of Israel after that time, declares the Lord. I will put my laws in their minds and write them on their hearts. I will be their God, and they will be my people. No longer will a man teach his neighbour, or a man his brother, saying, 'Know the Lord,' because they will all know me, from the least of them to the greatest (Heb. 8:10–11).

God yearns for us. It thrills Him to fully disclose Himself to us. At the heart of our relationship with God is knowing Him and being known by Him. We, too, want to be known and to truly know other people. Some people run from relationship to relationship, looking for that person who will understand them. The truth is that the only one who can do that completely and redemptively is God Himself. If we cut Him out of our life's equation, we will always long for some deeper comfort, some deeper commitment.

Our longing to know others and to be known by them originates from God's covenant design. Consequently, that longing cannot be fulfilled simply by relationships with other people. We can't expect any human to fill the space God reserved for Himself in our heart. That is why broken or unrealised covenant with God leaves us destitute in our psyche and impoverished in our soul and spirit.

God framed the world to work via relationship. His covenant with us is all about knowing Him and having relationship with Him. Remember that covenant relationship—the kind that offers the safety and emotional assurance necessary for full disclosure and intimacy—is established by God's sharing Himself with us. He offers His name and He shares His history with us. Covenant is all about communion with another. Its purpose is to offer us a lifelong opportunity to be deeply known.

Married Strangers

As we saw in the scenes at the beginning of this chapter, we want to be known and understood by those closest to us, those with whom we share covenant. That's why couples seeking divorce often claim:

> *We're strangers. We hardly talk. He doesn't know who I am any more, and I sure don't know who He is. I guess I've changed and matured. Maybe we didn't keep pace with each other. We have nothing in common except the kids, and we usually argue over them. Living with each other is like living with a stranger. That's not the kind of marriage I want to be stuck in for the rest of my life.*

Behind such accusations is the cry, 'I want to be with someone who wants to know who I am.' Deep down, we all

141

want to be known by the people we care about. When someone with whom we share a covenantal relationship doesn't value knowing and being known, we feel ripped off. We feel devalued as nothing more than the person who brings home the pay cheque, or the one who ferries the kids around or puts the meals on the table. Without the joy and the intimacy of being known, there seems little point to the relationship.

Danny and Heather
Longing to be known—if unfulfilled—can cause lots of problems in a marriage. It explains sudden meltdowns between couples. Donny and Heather are a classic case in point. I met with them at a restaurant for what I thought would be a social visit.

Before long, Heather got to the point: she asked me if I thought she was bitter. 'Why?' I asked.

After she and Donny exchanged guarded looks she told me: 'I've shut down sexually. Donny's touch is painful to me. I love him but I cannot respond to his advances.'

What puzzled them both was the suddenness of the change. I pointed out that the change was not sudden at all. It had been coming since their wedding night. It all had to do with her longing to be sought after and known by her husband; she interpreted his less-than-enthusiastic, methodical attempts at foreplay to mean that he did not want to know her.

For years she was the primary initiator of their physical intimacies. To test his interest, she refrained from initiating sexual activity for several days. He failed to pursue her, so she shut down. Her longing to be pursued and deeply known had a physical read out to it.

I helped Donny and Heather see something important about the other: they viewed sexual activity with different interest levels but also with different levels of meaning. He felt he had to live up to expectations he was afraid he couldn't meet; she felt he wouldn't abandon himself to pursue her.

The choice we make about whom to marry is part *romance*, part *physical attraction*, but mostly it is *desire to be fully known* by the one whom we wish to fully know. Romance creates feelings of specialness, vulnerability and anticipation. These feelings are all about wanting to know the one to whom we are attracted. Romance is the beginning of love and it acts like a magnet, drawing us to each other, and leading to full intimacy.

Romantic and physical attractions are preliminaries to the whole point of love: togetherness and intimacy. But romance can easily fade *after* you get to know someone well. That's why as a basis for marriage, covenant is better than romance. Covenant creates in each of its members a continual determination to know and to be known. We know we are loved when we feel our partner wants to keep knowing and accepting us.

We often lose contact with our covenant partner at a time of rapid transition in our lives. The start of a new job, the birth of a baby, the death of a parent, these are the times when the person involved is doing a lot of growing and learning about himself or herself. As spouses, it's our job to keep up with that growth.

Let's say a wife goes back to work after the children are in school. She learns a variety of new skills and enjoys many new experiences. Her new job is exciting. Her new workmates are interested in her ideas. But her husband? Instead of exploring her new world with her, he's plodding along the same old way he has for years, unwilling to share in the changes in her life. And when his wife leaves him he is completely surprised. He'll never understand what happened! It is vital that we keep listening to and learning from our spouse.

A Climate of Intimacy

No matter how long we've been married, our spouse should be confident that there is one person who knows and loves him or her. And if we want a strong and vibrant marriage, that person had better be us!

To flourish, our marriage requires a climate of intimacy like the one that God offers us. One where there is total forgiveness, and where the other party knows our heart is tender towards him or her, and that our desire is to do our spouse good. What are some hallmarks of such a climate? And how can we create it in our marriage?

Remember, you cannot force intimacy on others, nor can you demand it from them. You can only offer intimacy as an act of love. Love counteracts the sinful tendency to think primarily of yourself, because it constantly considers your loved one, not yourself.

In the redemptive order, love most often manifests itself in *forgiveness*. Unforgiveness disallows love. When you are unforgiving towards people, it chokes off your desire to do them good. You punish them for their wrongdoing; make them pay for what they have done to you. As long as you keep track of wrongs suffered, or hold on to the really bad things your spouse has said or done, you legitimise your choice to be unloving towards him or her.

Unforgiveness justifies its own hatred, anger, bitterness and self-pity, emotions that destroy intimacy. Unforgiveness acquaints us with our partner's sin rather than with our partner. Since it maintains separation, unforgiveness does as much damage as the wrong itself.

When things feel uncertain between husband and wife, it is hard for them to be vulnerable to each other. The more that husbands and wives cherish and value each other, the more they will be drawn together. Eager, consistent love is stimulating and unifying.

Trust is another important element for a climate of intimacy. The more consistent our responses and reactions are to each other, the more trust builds. Part of knowing our spouses is knowing what sorts of things to expect from them. Trust is built on what we know about each other. When that trust is betrayed, we feel we don't know who the person is any more. We think, *Who are you, and what have you done with my husband? The man I know could not do what you have done.*

Another key ingredient of intimacy is *humility*, or willingly admitting our faults to our spouse. Confession is powerful. In the bounds of covenant, true confession makes forgiveness fairly easy. When we confess, we must do three things. First, we must agree that what we did was *wrong*. If we offer reasons or justifications for our behaviour, we are not truly confessing. Confession says, 'I have no excuse for the *wrong* I have done.'

Second, we must agree that *we did indeed do* the wrong. If we blame others or claim that we were made to do it by some outside force, habit or peer pressure, we are not confessing. Confession says, 'I accept full responsibility for what *I have done.*'

Third, we must agree that what we have done has *violated others*. True confession acknowledges that our sin has created sorrow, loss or ruin for others. Confession says, 'The wrong I have done *has done wrong* to you.'

Children and the Intimate Question

The needs of children within the covenant relationship are not that different from those of husbands and wives. Remember Rayna, the teenager who accused her mother of not knowing who she was? How many of us remember that feeling? Children grow rapidly, and rather haphazardly, and unless we're careful to keep up with them, one day we will wake up and not know who it is we are living with.

We have already talked about the four parts of true covenant. Now I want to refocus our attention on the two beginning elements of covenant: *exchanging names* and *sharing history*. As we have learned, covenants are established between distinct individuals who call each other by name and who have extensive experience with each other. The point is that they know each other—well. And that is the reason children born into the covenant established by their parents will ask this most basic question of life: 'who am I?'

It is difficult to understand how it all works—how a child comes to a sense of personal identity within the context of family. Remember, family is a force, not just a description of physical relationships; the power of family is covenant—the setting God intended to bring great blessings to our lives. Family is a provision He gives to us, a tool He wants to utilise to do us good. God also means covenant to be a blessing to children.

In covenant, children intuitively ask, 'Do you know me?' Children presume that their parents can answer the question of their identity. They innately expect to be born into covenant. Long before children come to know themselves, they come to know people who know them.

Thus, our first question in life is often simply, 'Do you

know me?' Once children find those who know them, they have found covenant.

If children don't get a satisfactory answer from parents, or if they get a mixed message, they develop many anxieties. What's more, if Mum and Dad can't give the answer, the child looks to peer groups and to people who may or may not have a positive influence on their lives. When children look for someone who will take the time to know who they really are, they don't ask, 'Will you be a good influence on me', or, 'Are you the type of role model I need right now?' Instead, they simply ask, 'Do you know about me? Can you help me know myself?'

Tragically, many parents leave their children to figure out their identity on their own. But I can't teach myself who I am, because I don't know who I am. That is what parents do. Distortions exist in people's personalities when they have had to tutor themselves about who they are. Without adequate early instruction from family, children struggle with their identity most of their lives.

Family is supposed to say to every child, 'This is who you are and this is how you behave.' Whether or not parents intend to communicate that to family, it is communicated. When parents consciously or unconsciously refrain from telling their children about themselves, the children have a difficult time developing a meaningful sense of personal, particular identity.

You may never have heard your children say, 'Hey, Dad, who am I? Do I belong here?' But if you tune in your ear to hear the questions behind their questions, you *will* begin to hear it.

Our youngest, Evan, has not yet developed an understanding of time. The 'old days' to him are when Dad and the dinosaurs roamed the earth, and he always wants to know about way back when, when Dad was young. He wants to hear stories about me before he knew me.

But Evan and our other kids really love to hear stories about themselves before they knew themselves. It doesn't matter if the stories are kind of embarrassing. Hearing stories is like looking at their baby pictures. It fascinates them.

A few years ago, when Evan was four, someone returned the moses basket we loaned them. As I carried it into the garage, Evan asked me, 'What's that, Dad?'

'Honey, this is a moses basket,' I answered. 'Did you know this was your bed when you were a baby?'

He got a silly look on his face, and I could tell he was thinking, *No way could I ever have fitted in that.*

So I said, 'Yeah, you were such a cute little baby with nappies and rattles. That's right, you fitted in this thing. Can you believe that this is where you used to sleep—all snug and warm?'

He was intrigued. I was disclosing to him things about himself that he did not know. Telling him that he once was tiny somehow enlarged him by giving him more of himself. As I told him secrets about himself, he looked at me with a mischievous smile that seemed to mark me as a co-conspirator. It was almost as if he were saying, *We know a secret, Dad, don't we?*

Kids Look Through Our Eyes

At all ages, children want to know how we view them. They want to hear that they've always been a focal point, that they have always been known by us, and that they made enough impact on us for us to remember them.

Jan is one of four children, all of whom were born

within a five-year period. Her mother spent that part of her life in a blur of nappies and meal preparations. Years later when Jan asked her mother, 'How old was I when I began to walk?' or, 'What was the first thing I said?' her mother would start to answer and then say, 'No, wait a moment, I think that was your older sister. Or was it?' After a while, Jan got the message—her mother remembered the children *en masse,* but not as individuals. That was difficult for Jan. It was great to be one of the bunch, but she longed to be memorable for who she was.

Jan decided that she would not make the same mistake with her children, so she keeps an extensive photo diary for each of them. In it she records things she knows she could easily forget in the blur of her own motherhood experience. Interestingly, although the children are widely different ages, she frequently finds each one of them tucked in bed, looking at their book.

Ultimately, the power of family is not just to create biological offspring, but to give them a life patterned and shaped by the way we are towards them. Children are both the fruit of our loins and the fruit of our lips.

Telling Evan about himself was like introducing him to someone he had never met. By giving Evan a piece of his past, I secured something of his present. I made him more real to himself.

By communicating to our children that we do know them and by telling them stories about themselves, we build in them a security and comfort with themselves. Rather than telling children, 'This is who you are because I say so!', try story telling. By telling a story, we say, 'This is who you are because this is what you have been like.' If we do not tell our children what they have been, they will not know who they are.

One of a Kind

One of the greatest challenges we parents have is to see who our children are. They are different from each other, and it is our job to note those differences.

Hilary, our eldest, has always been conscientious. The way she faithfully sits at her desk and does her biology, history and maths homework doesn't surprise us at all. She likes working that way—methodically and persistently. Of all our children, she least minds doing a second, third or fourth draft of a school assignment.

I could have told you when she was three years old that would be the case.

She was fascinated by plastic bottles and caps—shampoo containers, washing-up liquid bottles, fabric softener jugs. Her favourite toys were about a dozen of these variously shaped and coloured plastic bottles. She lined the bottles up in a room one by one, with great precision and ceremony; she then unscrewed the caps and promptly reversed the process—over and over.

At the other end of the scale is Evan. He may grow up to be a stunt man, or work in sound-effects for movies. He has a noise for everything. His mum put plastic magnetic letters on the refrigerator door to help him learn to read. He soon turned them into fighting factions in a huge, explosive war.

It would have been easy to wish he were more like Hilary—but it would have devastated him! A huge challenge of parenting is to relinquish control in favour of guidance: to abandon the urge to dictate who our kids should be, and to uncover who they already are. The Bible tells us that each one of us is 'fearfully and wonderfully made'. We need to find that design, and then let our children know that we take delight in who they are.

Peering in the Mirror

Have you ever watched a child in front of a mirror? Children are fascinated by mirrors. They use them to fix their own image in their mind. Experimenting with themselves in the mirror, children make every imaginable twist of their face. They wonder what they will look like when they make strange faces. The mirror gives a simple answer.

Like a mirror, the primary responsibility of family is to present an adequate reflection of who a child is. Parents are adjustable mirrors who can move around to any angle and give children a glimpse of themselves—even the blind spots. Children's sense of who and what they are comes from what parents see in them. Parents can reflect almost anything to the child, and what a parent chooses to reflect determines how children see themselves.

If there is a dull reflection in the mirror—from disinterested parents—then children have to squint hard and stare intently to see who they are. Not getting much image response back from family creates insecure children. That insecurity can drive them to make exaggerated statements of personhood later in life. That is one reason why children *demand* so much attention. In all their attention seeking, they are trying to see a reflection of themselves.

Children need to see some kind of reflection. Looking in the mirror and seeing nothing is more frightening than looking in a mirror and seeing a rebellious child. If they see in the mirror a rebellious child, at least they can conclude that they are something, someone: 'Oh, that is who I am.'

Children see themselves as they are reflected in their parents' eyes. Peer pressure offers children the same service. People who are outside family covenant are not the ones to tell us who we are or what we ought to look like. But in dysfunctional homes, family fails as a mirror children can trust, because it gives them back either an ugly, distorted image or no image at all. Children will find mirrors. If family won't give them a meaningful reflection of who they are, they will seek that reflection elsewhere.

Adult Children of Uncomplimentary Parents

Children want to know what their parents think of them. What they see in the mirror of their parents' eyes, what they hear from their parents' lips frames their image of themselves. The implications of this are profound for their adult lives as well.

If children do not hear love, affection, attention and delight spoken into their souls, later in life those things will sound strange, unfamiliar and almost wrong. They will be uncomfortable with expressions of delight in them.

That's how Dottie felt. Through counselling with members of our ministry team, Dottie realised where all her discomfort and fear came from. She feared men in general, and male authority figures in particular. She never felt good about herself, and her only hope of measuring up came through what she could accomplish. She was tormented by rejection, self-hatred and an aversion to any physical contact with men—even kind hugs from men whom she knew were totally safe.

Dottie's father violated covenant with her. When she was a young teenager, her father allowed his male friends to joke about her physical development. He laughed and nodded approvingly when his friends made him promise—in her presence—to let them have her when she turned fourteen.

Obscene though the friends were, Dottie's father was the one who violated his daughter by not offering her protection. His garish grin and clouded eyes told her she was a 'thing,' a '*no*-thing'. Her value was no greater than a fat-tened calf to be sacrificed on the brutish altar of drunken men's lust.

Being loved by fellow church members and being told the truth about herself and her value as a person has helped Dottie to forgive her father. She is making a remarkable recovery from the dysfunctional family she grew up in. But think of the shame and embarrassment she experienced because of what her father said and did.

Much of the embarrassment people suffer over real intimacy—from the awkwardness they feel when gen-uinely complimented to the shyness they feel about their body—is a consequence of parents' failure to say to chil-dren, 'Yes, I know you, and I think you are wonderful.'

Adult children of uncomplimentary parents are tor-tured throughout life by a love-hate relationship with others' opinions about them. Compliment such adult chil-dren of affectionately dysfunctional families and you'll see them writhe and twist in pain. To escape the traumatic tangle of emotions a compliment produces, they laugh it off, ignore it or attribute sinister motives to the one who spoke it.

Such people feel ashamed to be complimented. They prefer to be told off, criticised or ignored rather than feel the awkwardness of being praised.

Likewise, people who were not made to feel special in their family will consciously rebut any compliment later in life with thoughts like: *That's not true. You are just saying that. What a lie. I know how ugly I am.*

All such thoughts effectively say the same thing: 'You don't really know me.' Why? Because children intuitively believe that their parents do know them—the real them. If parents did not compliment them, then they are not s upposed to be complimented. It isn't right because it wasn't done in family, the setting they came to believe was reality. Whoever compliments them must not really know them.

Thus, in tragic irony, other people's attempts at delightful intimacy with them get translated into proof that those people do not really know them. They think they must hide, because if people really knew what they are like (as defined for them by family), no one would want to be close to them. It is incomprehensible that anyone could delight in them, that anyone could find anything worthwhile in them.

The tragedy of dysfunctional families is not so much that they do not work properly, but that they imprint an identity image on their members that bears no resemblance to the person God meant them to be.

But that power of family can be changed for good. Our children will be forever marked by the impression we give them of themselves. What that impression will be is ours to decide.

9

Covenant: Sanctuary for Nurture and Growth

Remember those old black-and-white TV westerns? The ones where someone was always chasing someone else? To avoid being captured, the bad guys would escape into the safe sanctuary of the old country church. Within its sacred walls, the fugitives felt protected from the impending danger.

Covenant is a lot like that church. It's meant to be a sanctuary, a retreat, a haven where we will always find refuge and shelter. All of us need a safe place to grow, and covenant provides that place for us. Within its confines, sanctuary offers safety from pursuers and enemies. It is off limits to the local authorities because it is governed by a higher law. Sanctuary offers safety from the jurisdiction of laws that govern everything outside that sanctuary.

It is a world unto itself.

In the covenant we enter into with our heavenly Father, there is always the promise of safety—of ultimate sanctuary. Because of the commitment He has to us, we will always be safe with Him. Whatever happens to us, we can be sure that 'underneath are His everlasting arms.' Having covenant with God means simply this: He is always there, always with His heart towards us, always watching over us. We don't need to worry that God will love us one day and hate us the next, or whether He will be vindictive or petty with us. We have a consistent, ever-loving Father.

Within this restful place of covenant with God, we are free to grow spiritually. Think of the analogies that are drawn about Christians. We are trees planted by streams of water. Planted wheat that grows up to produce and multiply. Babies earnestly desiring the milk of God's word. Little children whose sins have been forgiven. All these word pictures imply growth and nurture. And that growth and nurture takes place within covenant with God. When we live in covenant, we are free to grow and mature. We see this in our relationship with God, as well as in our relationships with other people.

In my counselling, I've discovered that people having difficulty 'growing up' in certain areas of life often come from childhood families that did not provide for them a place of sanctuary. I remember Erica, who was married to a good, loyal husband. Still she could not completely trust him. When he had to be out at night, she constantly wondered whether he had told her the truth about where he was going. Although her anxieties were unfounded, they were wrecking her marriage. Love cannot grow well with roots of suspicion.

As Erica and I talked, I learned that she had never been trusted by her parents. They would give her permission to go somewhere or do something, then try to catch her in a lie about where she had been. In Erica's case, instead of her home being a place to grow into trust and independence, it was full of doubt. It's easy to see why she didn't trust her husband. Trust had not been modelled for her by her parents, and in turn, she found it almost impossible to relax and trust her husband.

The Agony of Uncertainty

One of the most important benefits of true covenant is certainty of relationship. It's having things settled once and for all—how I have been to you is how I will always be. No surprises or unexpected disclosures. No radical changes in behaviour or subtle shifts in standing.

Functional families offer that sort of emotional and psychological stability to their members. Of course, we all have an occasional bad day, but those temporary, individual changes from the norm should not make other family members nervous or frightened.

Without a stable family environment, trust cannot grow. Children find it hard to trust parents whom they cannot figure out. Children want to count on their parents. They need a constant reference point, and if they don't find that in their parents, they will seek it elsewhere.

In the safe covenant of family, children are not supposed to have to figure out their parents. Children forced into making sense out of their family environment—always trying to work out who Mum is today or what Dad is going to be like today—become tremendously disorientated.

Parenting is intentional—we determine to take care of our children. This means everything from preparing dinner to making sure the children have a pillow on their bed. Being a good parent requires continually evaluating what is going on in our children's lives, both physically and emotionally, and then responding to their needs. Not so with being a child. Children shouldn't have to constantly assess their parents' needs.

Children are traumatised by continual uncertainty. Worrying about whether a parent is going to be happy today or fly into a rage creates tension, because the child doesn't know how to act. Children's sense of who they are begins and is most greatly determined in their early years by relationship to people in their family.

Emotional and psychological exhaustion in adults often has its roots in a childhood that never felt secure. When players in the family drama shift from one characterisation to another, the children will handle their dismay by playing a role themselves. They will become either people pleasers, who adjust and blend in effectively no matter what, or rigid characters who can retain their identity despite the shifting cast.

Family members who relate to each other on the basis of contract instead of covenant will never fully develop as persons. We need freedom to experiment and explore within the boundaries of covenant if we are to fully realise our personhood. In marriage, we face dual challenges—individual growth, and growth as a couple. Sometimes a partner will feel he or she has 'outgrown' the other. Covenant provides opportunity for growth—together, not apart.

As a husband, I have to ask myself, 'Does my wife see me growing in maturity and wisdom as the years go by?' And, 'Am I ensuring that Pamela has the right environment in which to grow and be challenged?' In marriage, we can either encourage or discourage our spouse's potential. I know of wives who don't drive a car or balance the family budget because their husbands have convinced them they won't be able to do it to their satisfaction. Or husbands who won't attempt even the smallest household repair because their wives know they won't be able to fix things as well as their father did.

Contract relationships highlight shortcomings; covenant relationships encourage possibilities. As covenant partners, we, champion growth, new ideas and new experiences for our spouse. Are we their cheerleader, or are we the cork in their bottle? True covenant helps us develop every area of our lives to the fullest.

Sanctuary has an atmosphere—like a world within a world. The atmosphere of sanctuary that we call *family* is marked by absolute love and acceptance. Without this love and acceptance, children will be troubled the rest of their lives.

The Safety of Unconditional Love

Children are naturally curious. They try to figure out every-thing in their world. They channel their energies into exploring and forming questions that help them develop and learn. From the moment they can grasp an object, children go after anything within their reach. From hand to mouth they taste and examine all the data in their world, including telephone leads, spoons, rocks, blocks and shoes. Sights and sounds—from bright lights to sirens—become stimuli for their little minds to make sense of things.

Children who are well cared for—fed, rested, warm and changed—are naturally curious. The basic necessities provide a foundation that promotes curiosity. No wonder, then, that young school children cannot do well in class if they are hungry or poorly cared for. Life is more than food and shelter, but without them, children cannot learn and grow as they were meant to.

But children have another basic need: to be loved and to know it. Family is meant to provide that environment of unconditional love for children and parents alike. The safe environment of unconditional love means that the child is always certain how things stand. There is no uncertainty of relationship. Because love and acceptance are settled issues, the child feels free to explore life. As the child grows older, that security at home enables the adolescent to survey life without having to keep glancing back home to see how things are.

Secure, happy, well-adjusted children all have one thing in common—they know that they are loved. Feeling accepted by family removes the awkward self-consciousness felt by so many children and adults. When children feel rejected by parents, they fear rejection by people with whom they will want to establish relationship in the future.

Remember, babies are loved before they can *do* anything. In real family, children are conscious of being loved long before they are conscious of being. That we are loved and accepted is ultimately more important than merely being. The logic is so simple it almost escapes us. Being loved validates existence. Children who are secured by love from family are not vulnerable to insecurities about who they are.

There is a great difference between wondering what it is about us that others *do* love and wondering whether there is anything in us others *could* love. *Being* loved and *feeling* that love makes self-discovery delightful. Not knowing whether we are loved makes self-discovery frightening and agonising. Children who do not feel loved intuitively fear discovering why—what horrible thing makes them so unlovable?

Parents as Filters

Parents provide a stable environment of love for children to explore their uniqueness. But that's not all. Parents are also to be filters, interpreters to our children of the subtleties of life. Emotions, attitudes and thoughts swirl around in a child's head and heart. We can help them by naming and explaining those thoughts and emotions.

One of our children struggles with self-pity. We have

been working on this now for many months, trying to help our child see the difference between feeling sad and feeling sorry for oneself. We use this question to help the child clarify the difference: do you want others to join you in feeling sorry? Self-pity is when you think that other people should feel as bad for you as you feel for yourself. Self-pity basically says, 'Well if you aren't going to feel sorry for me, someone has to, so I will feel sorry for myself.' We don't want our children to be unaware of what self-pity is, so we explain the difference between sadness and self-pity.

Whenever I return from a lengthy trip, I try to bring my children some little surprise to communicate that I love them and that I thought about them while I was gone. Understandably, then, when I arrive home the children always want to know, 'What did you bring me, Dad?' Acquisitive little dears, aren't they? Over time, we demonstrate to children how to be sensitive to the person who is giving a gift. But you can't say to a three-year-old, 'Don't be so greedy.' Instead, we interpret that subtlety to them.

It will take a while, but when my children finally leave home, I want them to be able to identify and to understand different emotions. Those emotions experienced later in life become landmarks—signposts to tell adult children where they are. I want my children to be able to say, 'Oh yes, that is self-pity, and I learned a long time ago that if I go that way, I will get stuck.' I want my children to know how to find their way back home through the tangle of feelings and motives.

Parents as Calibrators

Another responsibility of parents is to calibrate their children's internal emotional, psychological and spiritual instruments. To *calibrate* means to align everything so that

161

it gives accurate readings or measurements. We calibrate externally all the time. For instance, remember the last time you pulled out the bathroom scales to assess the damage from dinner? Before you got on the scales, you may have noticed the red line was not on zero. Calibrating the scales means adjusting them to zero. If the scales aren't calibrated properly, the reading will be misleading.

This is how it is for children. Their perspective on how important they are in life sometimes requires parental adjustment. Maybe your child feels his or her whole world is falling apart. As a parent, you say, 'Now, it's not that bad. Everything will be OK.' Instinctively, parents bring proper perspective to their children's experiences. Without correct calibration, children are left with wild extremes of emotions. Parents have the authority and power (rather, the privilege and responsibility) to interpret signals and adjust perspective in their children.

Children need calibrating. Without it, their childish interpretation of the world goes unchallenged. For example, when my son, Collin, loses a soccer game, he wants to blame someone else. He usually tells me how unfairly the other team played or how bad the officiating was—stories I never hear when he wins. As a parent, my role is to empathise with him and affirm his play on the field, but I must also help him to see the whole picture. I need to tactfully challenge his assumption that the referee was 'out to get them'.

If I agree with Collin that he would have won the game if the play and the officiating had been fair, I encourage him to become a resentful excuse maker, rather than a man who learns to enjoy the game, whether he wins or loses.

This incredible power is one more evidence of how

family can so radically and permanently affect children. Distortion and confusion result when parents incorrectly calibrate their children's consciences, their sense of right and wrong or what is real. The common psychological term for this is *denial*—families simply refusing to acknowledge real frustrations or behaviours.

When Mum and Dad have been fighting, children intuitively sense danger in the family sanctuary. If parents deny what is happening by glibly telling children that everything is OK, children must choose between believing their parents or their feelings. Even worse is when parents deny abusive behaviour, alcoholism, persistent rage or frustration.

My point is, what is normal at home becomes what children expect as normal, period. If we will fix the delicate internal instruments in our children and calibrate them according to what is good, true and honourable, our children will forever seek to return to the readings they remember from their childhood.

Conversely, if we calibrate their perceptions incorrectly we set them up to stumble again and again. That was the case with Margaret—an incredibly efficient, talented woman whose inner expectations of herself always left her feeling that she could not measure up. She was more comfortable being disappointed with herself than being pleased with herself. Why? Her family had always focused on what she couldn't do.

How we parent our children affects them their entire lives. What they see now is what they'll return to as adults. Why do people stay in marriages where physical or verbal abuse regularly occurs? There are many complex issues at work, and I don't mean to over-simplify it, but if you were to interview those abused people, you would find that they were calibrated to accept abuse as part of life. They learned to live with it as a child. It was 'normal' to them. Therefore, when abused as adults, they did not know to say, 'There's more to life than this. No one has the right to do this to me. Good-bye.' Unfortunately, abuse is normal for them.

We protect our children from emotionally hellish situations as adults by ensuring that if they ever stepped into one by accident, it would be so alien to them that they would step straight out of it again.

As we're beginning to see, parenting goes far beyond administering discipline. Our privilege and responsibility is to set the 'normal' range for our children's emotional gauges. Sometimes that means telling them a disappointment isn't the end of the world. At other times it may mean recalibrating our own emotions so we can 'weep with those who weep'. Understanding the awesome power and responsibility of correctly calibrating my children's emotions makes me want to get my act together, to deal with the 'stuff' from my past.

Ultimately, we are to treat our children so that they have no trouble believing God is kind, loving, gentle and merciful, and that He exerts all of His influence and power and authority to do good to His children all the days of their lives.

Safe and Holy

Another equally important component of offering our children a sanctuary in which to grow and mature is giving them boundaries that will keep them safe. Children cannot reach their potential in an unsafe environment. That's why little ones don't get to play with matches, or wander on the road, or swing from the railing on the eighth-floor landing. It isn't safe.

So we train them, until one day they can be left alone in a room with matches because they understand the dangers of fire. They not only cross the road, eventually they get to drive on it. But by the time they do, hundreds of hours of road safety will have been drilled into them. These boundaries keep our children safe.

To those of us who value our families and live covenantally with them, family sanctuary is a holy place. Parents have been charged by God to nurture and train their children in the way they ought to go. Becoming a family is not something that I take upon myself because I decide to have children. Family is a spiritual reality. A holy thing.

What does it mean that family is holy? It means that family has a special reality, a sacred certainty to it. It provides emotional and relational boundaries, so that if children stay inside them, they are safe. Outside those boundaries, they are vulnerable to pursuers and to enemies of their soul.

The danger, of course, comes when parents use the sanctuary of family for themselves—to protect their own selfish, distorted world—rather than providing a healthy world for their children. The covenant family is a *safety* for children and a *sacrifice* for parents. In an unsafe atmosphere, a child's inner person remains dwarfed and undeveloped. To reach their full potential, children must feel safe.

We keep our children emotionally safe by giving them clear boundaries. They need to be told what is safe and what is not. Because the lines between safe and unsafe emotional boundaries have become blurred, it is imperative we find our standards in God's Word.

Family as Womb

Covenantal family is meant by God to act for children in the same way the womb acts for the unborn. For example, womb-children are unable to feed themselves, and are unconsciously nourished by the mother. What she eats eventually passes through her digestive system and through the umbilical cord to the baby. The foetus does not evaluate what comes through Mum. If Mum ingests toxins, they pass to baby through the same avenues as nutrients do. Pregnant women have to watch what they eat lest their utterly dependent child suffers dangerous consequences from dangerous substances.

The same is true in family. Children are made by God to openly take in what comes through Mum and Dad. Parents feed children far more than food. Mums and dads who provide a sensible diet of healthy communication and nurture ensure that their children will grow to be well fed and strong.

But children fed the wrong sort of diet—anger, neglect, abuse, lovelessness—will be malnourished and ill-prepared to face the rigours of life.

Babies were not made to be exposed too early to the elements of their new world. The womb is where they develop sufficiently to face what is coming. That, too, is what family is supposed to do for children. The family covenant protects children from the challenges, complexities and competitions of adulthood until the children are ready to handle them.

Sin has a sting to it. Like a scorpion's tail, sin whips out at anyone in its reach with deadly venom. Adults can withstand far more poison without suffering significant damage than children. Family keeps away all the scorpions it can. The music we let our children listen to, the videos we allow them to watch had better not violate the covenant statement we make to them in the sight of God.

Rather than holding them back or thwarting their creativity as some therapists suggest, giving our young children a protected environment assures their emotional and mental health. *Protected* does not imply *restrictive* or *harsh,* but an environment free from dangerous elements.

When a premature baby dies, the medical doctor knows immediately. But it is difficult for a psychologist to pinpoint the moment a daughter's innocence died or a son was traumatised by some vulgarity he was too young to withstand. Covenant parents promise to carry their children to 'full term', to protect them from choices, activities and exposures that are deadly to their still developing psyches.

Recently, I read a nationally syndicated advice column for teenagers. An eighteen-year-old girl wanted some feedback. She wrote:

> *I'm a good student and don't do drugs, alcohol or tobacco. But I am sexually active with my boyfriend and have been for over two years, and I'm very proud of it. So is my mother, who encouraged me to get into a sexual relationship when I was sixteen, so I wouldn't have sexual hang-ups when I get married. I know you are not in favour of premarital sex but I am living proof that it can be successful. I did have an abortion last year, but we use full protection now and it will never happen again.*

This mother has offered her daughter a new world where there is no one to tell her no. And what has her daughter gained so far? Sexual expertise at age sixteen, a few thrills and the superiority of knowing she can 'go all the way'. But what has she lost? Her virginity. The chance to approach sex within the bounds of maturity and the safety of covenant. She has lost her first born child, trading the joy of giving birth to a longed-for baby, for the cold reality of an abortion clinic. And, since she did not use proper protection there is the possibility of AIDS developing in the years to come. Yet after only two years, she declares the whole venture a resounding success.

This girl's mother abdicated her role as her daughter's emotional and spiritual supervisor in favour of allowing her, maybe even coercing her, to experience things for which she was not ready.

Children need help knowing when they are ready for new experiences. I have never heard any of my children say, 'Dad, thanks for the offer, but I don't think I'm old enough to handle the consequences of doing that yet.' Children are not realistic about what they can handle. Often, tragically, they can determine that only from hindsight. They lack the big picture—the perspective that comes with years of experience. We parents can see the big picture, and are obliged to use that knowledge to direct our children. If we fail to do so, we fail them.

Functional family is supposed to carry and support children long before they can carry themselves. Once again, our everyday language alerts us to truth. We talk about children learning to take responsibility and learning how to *carry themselves* in life. Children learn to *carry themselves* in life by how they are carried by their parents. Sometimes, carrying a child in family involves physically drawing him or her close in our arms. But mostly, carrying is an emotional posture parents adopt towards their children. In the process we send all manner of signals to our children about how they should eventually carry themselves.

If we are careful with our children, they will carry themselves carefully as adults. If we are gentle with them, they will be gentle with themselves and with others. If we 'drop' them often or grow tired of 'putting up with them', they, too, will become frustrated with and neglectful of themselves and others when they are grown.

When our children face inevitable disappointments—skinned knees, failed assignments, missed soccer goals, best friends moving out of town or broken hearts—how we support them makes all the difference in how they continue to develop in their personality and character. As time goes by, our children will need us less and less. They'll get over the skinned knee before we know it. Soon they'll snuggle in our arms only rarely, and never long enough.

But they will have learned in family what it is to be carried in the heart. And one day those little arms, now grown so big and strong, will carry us.

Guarding the Sanctuary

I cannot protect my children from all physical harm. Neither can I shield them from all the sadness of life. But as a parent, God has given me incredible power to protect my children from a great many spiritual, emotional and psychological traumas. To do that, I must give them ample instruction and opportunity to learn where the boundaries are, without being arbitrary, harsh or inconsistent.

Boundaries we give our children should not be merely for our convenience. We set boundaries for children to keep them from being hurt. Boundaries established for the good of the parent, rather than for the good of the children, are illegitimate. Such boundaries map out the borders of a distorted family. God doesn't establish boundaries in our life for His benefit. He establishes them all for us.

When the power to set family boundaries is misused, horrors such as child abuse are possible. A child intuitively knows who is boss. Parents establish the rules in the home that's the way it is. So, when a father caught up in his own wickedness and distortion sexually abuses his daughter, something inside the little girl sends off alarm bells. And yet the other part of her says, 'This is Dad, and he makes the rules.' She has no choice but to do what she's been told.

Yet, she senses something is very wrong. When she grows older and finally comprehends that she has been betrayed by her father, she concludes that she cannot trust authority. She learns that offers of safety are probably only traps for exploitation. Her dysfunctional upbringing leaves her suspicious of all male authority figures, but also tragically vulnerable to being preyed upon sexually by men. Her father *teaches* her how to deal with men and what to expect from life. Her identity and her hope for survival are enmeshed in a perverse tangle of sexuality, discomfort, betrayal and alarm.

A sanctuary offers safety, not ambush. The legitimacy of a sanctuary, indeed, its whole purpose, is protection and refuge. An unsafe sanctuary is dysfunctional. The sanctuary of family becomes unsafe when parents ignore the higher law of God in their family, and make their own laws. Unholy sanctuaries always create distortions. In family, a child wonders, 'Can I trust you? Can I trust that you are not going to violate me? Can I trust that you are going to tell the truth? Can I trust that you will really tell me the way that life is?'

In real family, the answer is *yes*.

10

Recovering from Broken Covenant

The more we see that God meant family to prosper and to secure its members, the more we become aware that our families did not do that for us. We then have the bewildering task of determining what went wrong in our upbringing and why we have ended up as we are.

We could blame ourselves for everything. After all, we are the most consistent element in our life; at every point when we made wrong choices or did inappropriate things, we were there. We get down on ourselves and lapse into ugly self-hatred.

Recently, I saw this in Colleen, a bright young mother and devoted wife. Colleen had a hard time trusting God. She was afraid she wouldn't measure up to what God required of her. A legalist, she expected life to add up according to a formula something like this: *I can't handle life completely on my own; I cannot do for myself.* (Sounds accurate so far.) *God will grant me grace only if I am good enough, smart enough or sincere enough. Therefore, if God does not come through for me, the fault must be mine.*

It bugged Colleen that she couldn't be good enough for God, so she alternated between self-hatred and self-pity. It wasn't until Pamela and I talked with Colleen that she saw how her 'works mentality' (thinking that God extended grace only to good enough people) short-circuited God's grace. God will not come through for Colleen on her terms because He does not want her to keep believing that she has to *work* for His grace.

Where did Colleen develop this mentality? From her perfectionistic and highly critical mother and distant, workaholic father. Dad was rarely around—mostly only on special occasions—so Colleen looked forward to birthday parties, Christmas Eve and other big events. But even when her father was there, he wasn't attentive to her. Meanwhile, Colleen's mother always fussed over the little things in everyone's life. Nothing was ever good enough. Colleen never measured up.

The hurt in our lives, the reason we are the way we are, is the result of how we were raised. Families framed by contracts rather than covenants, or families that violated any of the elements of covenant, produce traumatised and wounded children. The question then is: how can we recover from a broken covenant?

I must caution against another extreme response that is as empty as blaming ourselves. It does us no good to transfer blame to our parents. I don't point these things out so that we can blame parents and excuse ourselves for our own sins. Attributing blame and pointing a finger at someone else rarely accomplishes what we want it to. We must be careful of any therapy or counselling that shifts culpability onto others and leaves it there.

Whom then, shall we blame? How can we ever be free of our traumas and addictions if we cannot lay them at another's feet?

Honouring Parents

God wants all of us to be healed from the consequences of

broken covenants. The first step in restoring our life from the bruises and traumas of covenant violation is to *forgive* others—not to blame them. This is especially true of our parents.

But we face a dilemma when our parents did and said hurtful things to us. God doesn't tell us to pretend that everything our parents did was right. He isn't arguing for some kind of perverse denial. He is aware that parents have done cruel and wicked things to their children—cursing, violating, ignoring and rejecting them. How can such parents be honoured? Should we lie to ourselves and to others by claiming we had great parents?

The answer is not to deny or excuse our parents' unintentional mistakes or their wicked behaviour. The answer, instead, is to take care that we do not sin as a consequence of their sin. Just because our parents neglected or violated God's commands does not mean that we now have licence to violate them also. Sin always results in trauma to the human soul; sin never heals the soul. Bitterness, unforgiveness and dishonour towards parents are every bit as deadly as parental abuse. Though our natural reaction to someone's sin against us is to sin against them, Jesus calls us to another way. He tells us not to take our own revenge, but to turn the other cheek instead.

Saul and David

Although appointed by God as king, Saul lost his authority because he disobeyed God's direction to utterly destroy the Amalekites. Saul's own disobedience to God created a vengeful attitude towards David. Having begun a life-style of self-determination and rebellion, Saul tried to maintain his authority and standing with others by his own efforts. He forfeited godly authority and sought to impose his own.

I've discovered that people who become abusive authorities often have knowingly disregarded things that God told them to do. Living in rebellion, without the true authority of spiritual perception, they hold on to their place of power by exercising distorted force in the lives of other people. Abuse is born out of frustration. When people put aside God's patterns of obedient servanthood and attempt to secure their standing by their own hands, they abuse authority. God gives authority for the sake of others—to build them up and to release them to the full measure of their destiny in God.

Saul was David's father-in-law. Yet Saul repeatedly tried to murder David. I think you'll agree that attempted murder of a family member qualifies as abuse. Saul was an abuser, and David his intended victim. Twice, David had opportunity to take matters into his own hands by killing Saul. But knowing God's way, he chose *not* to take revenge. David would not violate precepts of his covenant with God in order to secure himself from his abuser. That was Saul's sin—disregarding God's commands and protecting himself. David chose to place himself in God's hands rather than rebelliously deliver himself with his own hands. God then made a way for David to escape his abuser.

Some years later, Saul died. David's response seems strange to us. Instead of celebrating his abuser's death, David mourned. He separated Saul, the abuser, from Saul, the authority in his life.

This is the first step in recovering from our past so that it ceases to shape our future. Hard to do, difficult even to imagine, but instead of celebrating our abuser's demise, we must mourn their loss from our lives.

You don't have to subject yourself to their abuse while they are alive. If your parents have been abusive towards you, I'm not suggesting you maintain a close relationship with them. David distanced himself from Saul, and stayed away for years. But physically fleeing for safety is different from longing for revenge. David's desire to save his own life was not the same as thoughts of vengeance and taking his abuser's life.

David recognised that killing Saul, who had been given a place of godly authority in his life, would be rebellion against God. Have people who have been given authority over us (like parents) violated covenant and done us harm instead of good? We will never find God's plan for our recovery if we allow a spirit of revenge and hatred to occupy our soul.

Saul tried to murder David. If David had tried to murder Saul, he would have been as guilty as Saul. 'But he deserved to be killed. Look at how wicked he was. Look at what he did to ruin David's life.' These judgements against Saul sound so right, like our judgements against our own parents. But they will never offer us recovery. When we take revenge, a subtle and insidious form of self-justification creeps into our soul.

It works like this: because we are fairly decent people, we do not allow ourselves to kill someone without reason. That would be murder—the highest level of abuse. So, in order to feed the murderous thoughts in our minds, we must judge that our intended victim is evil beyond redemption. We justify our hateful attitudes by assuring ourselves that *he or she deserves it.* That is why it is hard for us to find anything that may have been good about an abusive parent. Our soul does not want to acknowledge anything good about that parent because if we did, we could not continue to justify our desire to murder him or her.

Songs of Celebration

To mourn Saul's passing, David sang a song celebrating Saul's good qualities. To be finally free from past abuse—especially by our parents—we must, like David, separate *what* they did to us from *who* they are (redeeming qualities) and from *the place* God positioned them in our lives. 'There is nothing good about my father' is a convenient lie that justifies our desire to avenge what happened to us. The lie may sustain deep anger in our soul, but it will not heal the wounds.

If you want to experience recovery, find something about your abuser to be thankful for and to sing about. Thank your parents for birth, shelter, food or a work ethic. Stand facing the ocean waves or in the quiet midst of a forest and sing a simple heartbreaking song of celebration about the good in your parent. And sing of all the good there might have been if your parent had properly used covenant in your life.

We honour our parents by acknowledging the weight of the role they play in our lives. It does not mean that we think everything they did to us was right or good. To honour does not mean to say our parents were always right. To honour means to recognise that our parents have a unique and weighty place in our lives—a place made for them by God. They may have abused that God-given role when they abused us. But we will likewise abuse it if we dishonour them.

I have found this principle helps people from dysfunctional families learn to honour their parents. Find things about your parents and the way you were raised that you can be thankful for, and acknowledge their God-given place in your life. You cannot simply dismiss them from your life or wipe them away. Remember, unforgiveness will make their sins loom so large that you will be tempted to say you have nothing to be grateful for. And self-pity is eager to tell you that you would have been better off never being born. Resist those justifications and ask God to show you the parts of your family experience that were good.

Additionally, it may help you in the honouring/forgiving process towards your parents to acknowledge that much of what they did to bruise your soul was a consequence of how they, themselves, were traumatised by their upbringing. The Bible refers to the 'desolations of generations' (Isa. 61:4), and reminds us that children and grandchildren do 'as their fathers did' (2 Kings 17:41). What was done to your parents explains much of what they did to you. The more we can say, 'Forgive them, they didn't know what they were doing', the easier it will be to honour our parents. Our parents were wounded, too.

Most of the harm parents do to their children results from ignorance, not determined violation. In most cases, they did the best they knew how with us—as we are trying to do with our own children. We must be careful not to attribute sinister motives to parents who simply acted with imperfect understanding. Imperfect parents are not necessarily abusing parents. All of us are broken people living in a broken world. It should not be surprising that parenting is done inadequately. As the Bible says, our parents instructed us 'for a little while as they thought best' (Heb. 12:10)—a tacit acknowledgement that they will not do it perfectly.

Ray and Sylvia

As often happens, I counselled both a father (Ray) and his

daughter (Sylvia)—not at the same time, but about the same issue: their fathers. Ray's description of his father, Earl, a career military man, and their relationship was bleak and depressing. Earl ran his home with military efficiency and expected no-nonsense obedience. Ray got as much affection at home as a raw recruit got in basic training.

Because the family moved a lot, Ray gave up on establishing close relationships with friends or schoolmates. He simply endured the long, lonely days and left home—to enter the military—as soon as he was old enough to escape his father. He took with him the nervous anxiety, aloofness and heartbreak you would expect to find in one who was raised like that. Ray didn't know how to relate to himself, much less to anyone else.

Eventually, Ray married. When I met him, he was in his early forties. Four years after Ray and his family started coming to our church, I learned that his daughter Sylvia was nearing an emotional breakdown. She was angry, rebellious, frightened and immobilised to the point that she would curl up in a foetal position for hours each day. When I heard about Sylvia, I felt prompted by the Lord to focus on her relationship with her father, Ray.

Sure enough, her complaints against her father sounded like a recording of Ray's heartbreak over his father: aloof, commanding, insistent and unaffectionate. Once I pointed out to Ray that he was doing the very things his father had done to him, Ray repented and asked his daughter's forgiveness. Both father and daughter are well on their way to recovery now because they were able to find compassion for each other.

It may help you honour and forgive your parents if you realise that your pain closely matches theirs. Mercy towards them will lessen the pain to you. This is the secret of forgiveness. Forgiving others is the surest therapy for abuse.

Forgiveness

Without forgiveness there can be no recovery from the effects of dysfunctional family in our life. Forgiveness is not some benign act of weakness, nor is it trivialising the sin committed. Forgiveness is the most fundamental dynamic in God's redemptive plan to heal a broken planet. Forgiveness counteracts the damage of violated covenant. That is why God sent Jesus to extend forgiveness to the same people who violated His covenant. Without forgiveness, both the violated one and the violator stay stuck in the grip of what has happened. Forgiveness offers a new future to both, but especially to the victim.

Forgiveness is powerful and awe-inspiring. The power to forgive supersedes the power to judge, and that is why mercy triumphs over judgement. The Bible says of God, 'But with you there is forgiveness; therefore you are feared' (Ps. 130:4). Forgiveness has the final say, and thus, the highest place. Juries pronounce guilt. Judges set sentences. But none of them has the power of the pardon granter. Governors and heads of state have power to grant pardons to convicted criminals.

Although it pretends to grant us a sense of moral superiority, unforgiveness actually offers little power over our abuser. As long as we are unforgiving, we are *reacting* to the sin committed against us. The sin plays over and over in our minds because that is the nature of unforgiveness. It cannot let the sin go, it cannot leave the sin behind. Unforgiveness always leads to a future consumed by the past. It becomes a sick recycle of the past, being engulfed not only by what actually happened, but by the replays of what took place.

Unforgiveness won't let us get beyond what happened. Ultimately, we are ravaged more by unforgiveness than by the grievance. Unforgiveness heightens our traumas rather than diminishing them. It never soothes or heals the hurts. It gives false promises of satisfaction, empty boasts of empowering us over the agonies to which we must submit.

Sometimes we hesitate to forgive because we worry that the person who did something to us will 'get away with it'. We want our unforgiveness to act as a psycho-emotional bounty hunter that will bring the guilty party to justice. Let me say two things about this. First, *only guilty people can be forgiven.* Forgiveness proclaims guilt, it does not deny it. By forgiving our parents for the way they may have violated covenant with us, we do not say they did not violate it. We don't pretend it never happened. We don't forget about it.

We do the only righteous thing we can with their sin; we *mark* it by *forgiving* it. The moment we forgive, it ceases to mark us. By forgiving their sin, we remove its power over us. We cease to be the victim. When Joslyn's father sexually abused her, she was his victim. Every time she relived that abuse through unforgiveness, she continued as the victim. Once she forgave her father, she was no longer subject to his victimisation. He was still guilty of the sin, but she was no longer victimised by it.

Second, *forgiveness frees us from a common fate with the guilty.* Jesus warns us not to judge others, because we will trigger judgement on ourselves. All judges are judged. Only God can judge with impunity. When the same measure of judgement that He uses against the earth is applied to Him, no unrighteousness is found in Him. Not so with us. When we judge others and condemn them, we condemn ourselves. Unintentionally, we assign a common fate to us both.

Since recovery and redemption are based on forgiveness and grace, rather than merit and law, we cannot hope for personal recovery without forgiveness. A victim mentality claims that we would be fine if only we had not been traumatised by parents or others. That isn't true. Though covenant violation may have exacerbated the dysfunctions in our soul, our own sins have been more than enough cause for damage to our being. Even without being violated, we are needy souls crying out for forgiveness.

We have violated covenant with God. Only his grace and forgiveness can restore what we have lost by that violation. If we refuse to forgive those who have violated covenant with us, then we prevent God from forgiving us. Unforgiving victims and unforgiving victimizers share a common fate: they must make do without grace. That is why Jesus teaches us to pray, '. . . forgive our trespasses as we forgive those who trespass against us' (Matt. 6:12).

Every time God pronounces guilt, He offers forgiveness. He convicts us of sin, then once we acknowledge its existence, He gladly washes it away by the blood of Jesus Christ. That is the essence of the New Covenant. Yes, God judges, but He extends forgiveness after the judgement. Judgement without forgiveness is not God's type of judgement. Nor does God forgive without judging. If we want to recover from the effects of a dysfunctional family, we must forgive our family.

Redeeming the Past

One of the most profound promises in the Bible is God's pledge to restore us—to wholeness, to peace, to prosperity of soul—and to redeem the years of our past that have been ravaged. He does this not by having us relive our life without its traumas, but by freeing us from the effects of our past. This means that we can look forward to a life determined not by our past family upbringing, but by our present obedience.

As I have already pointed out, however, a functional future necessitates that we walk according to God's ways, not our own ways. God redeems through powerful spiritual tools—love, submission, sacrifice, obedience, grace, forgiveness, repentance. Once we determine to join in with Him in redeeming our past, He instructs us in how to do it. Spiritual and biblical counsel from your church or a trustworthy friend will help you navigate the particulars of God's plan for you.

Rejection and Low Self-Esteem

We should mention two common effects of a broken covenant with parents. When family covenant dissolves, the children's whole world is shattered—their sense of what is right, their sense of continuity and roots, their understanding of themselves. Nothing is as it was. No matter what the issues between Mum and Dad, a child can only interpret divorce as abandonment and covenant breaking.

Studies indicate that children often blame themselves for divorce. That explains the temporary personality disorders experienced by children after a divorce. That is reality, and I don't dispute it. But I want to add some thoughts about what *else* happens to children and to spouses when covenant is broken.

Whether or not the parents of a dysfunctional family divorce, children of a family that has broken covenant with its members feel rejected. They sense the parents' fundamental refusal to have them, to take them or to hold them. Children feel rebuffed and discarded, even if the parents don't intentionally act that way towards the children.

Broken covenant is like a broken container: everything it once held drains out of the cracks. Thus, the children face a passive ejection from family that ultimately makes them feel vaguely disqualified for life and uneasy with themselves.

The feeling of rejection is compounded by low self-esteem because children learn to value themselves according to how they are valued in covenant family. Self-esteem is not self-determined or self-taught. We do not establish our own worth. If the important people in our lives do not demonstrate interest in, use for or delight in us, we conclude that we have little value. Parents who break covenant rob their children of self-esteem. Though those children may try later in life to convince themselves they are really valuable, they rarely succeed.

Trying to build our own self-esteem is self-defeating. If we do not esteem ourselves, we will not value our own opinion, so even if we tell ourselves that we are significant, our words carry little weight. We come to conclusions about ourselves based on the evidence of how others feel about us. Family imprints our value on our soul. Broken covenant leaves children feeling like damaged goods.

Rejection and low self-esteem are normal reactions to a broken covenant. Feeling guilty about feeling rejected only compounds the difficulty of recovery. But we do not want to live with rejection and low self-esteem. How can we recover from them?

Remember God's Covenant

Let's not forget that the family covenant is not the only covenant we are in. If we have opened our heart to the love of God in Jesus Christ, we have been drawn into a New Covenant—one that He will never break with us. He never forsakes or rejects us. He always stays with us. He welcomes, adores and receives us to Himself.

Our covenant with God does not replace the violated covenant with our family, it supersedes it. By faith we choose to believe what God says of us is true. The more we contemplate His sacrificial love for us and the more we understand how Jesus endured rejection to redeem the world, the more we will experience recovery from our own rejection. God places inestimable value on us. The more important He becomes in our lives, the more weight His opinion about us has. Honouring Him restores our sense of value.

None of us can be our own saviour. Sincerity, determination, effort and willpower will not compensate for violated covenant. But another covenant, a stronger covenant, has the same type of power to secure us as the broken covenant had to reject us. Since God's covenant with us is greater than our covenant with our family, its power to heal is greater than any damage done to us by the weaker covenant that was broken. The power of God's family can more than compensate for the losses we suffered in our own family. The secret is to access the provisions of God's covenant with us by living according to the patterns of life He has called for in that covenant.

Refuse the Comfort of the Victim

In his book *A Nation of Victims,* Charles Sykes charges that our culture recommends that we take no responsibility for our condition, but that we blame people or forces for keeping us where we are. True, people we love have done bad things to us. It does us no good to pretend that our relationships are fine when they are not. But we must be careful not to stay stuck as a victim in the same way we were stuck in denial.

There is something profoundly beguiling about being a victim. It frees us from the need to change or struggle against the sinful attitudes that engulf us. As we saw earlier, our legitimate sorrow over being wounded can easily become an illegitimate excuse for hateful, vengeful thoughts. Having a victim mentality means that if we can find someone to blame for our condition, we are free to give up. It keeps us from embracing the future God has for us and keeps us focused instead on the past.

When we are first victimised, we have no choice. Someone—perhaps a parent or a spouse—does something to us without our permission. That is what a victim is, someone who suffers through no fault or choice of their own. A victim is taken advantage of by another.

Remaining a victim, though, is partially a choice we make. We may feel it inevitable because it is difficult to move towards change by acknowledging that we have been emotionally or psychologically traumatised by an abuser. Denial must be overcome if we are to experience recovery. But to stay there will keep us cornered. Remaining a victim presents false comforts and securities. Its creed is as follows: *No one can blame me if I stay as I am. Since this was done to me, now I want things done for me. No one understands how I have been hurt. My sin is nothing compared to their sin. I will not forgive. I will not repent. I will not submit. I must defend myself.*

Victims believe their own sins are justified by the sins committed against them. True recovery cannot come to people who choose to remain victims. We must take responsibility; acknowledge that our own sins of unforgiveness, bitterness and revenge are as evil as the sins committed against us; walk ahead in obedience; and seek to bring glory to God.

It sounds hard, but it will set us free.

Spouse of a Broken Covenant

Breaking covenant always breaks people. Members of the broken covenant often retreat into another covenant type of relationship, in hopes of finding the security and familiarity they crave. Generally, people do not break one covenant until they have at least started negotiations on another one.

Thus, unless she has been driven away by severe violation, a woman usually will not leave her family until she has the prospect of another bonding, a new relationship, a job—something. Likewise, the husband who deserts his wife and kids usually does not do so to be alone. He deserts one covenant to pursue another. There is another woman, his career, alcohol—something else to which he plans to bond.

A covenant breaker never *just leaves*. He or she always goes to some other place or some other person that promises a better covenant than he or she has had.

The ones left behind, however, do not benefit from a preplanned retreat elsewhere. They are left with a fragmented world. The 'left' ones often retreat into covenant with the one they know will offer it to them immediately—themselves.

Thus, people who have been shoved out of covenant relationship with spouse or parent hastily make all sorts of promises to themselves to never again do this and that. They swear to themselves and bind themselves with oaths. Sometimes these oaths are angry and bitter. Other times they are pitiful and resigned.

But they are always dangerous and destructive.

Recovery from a broken covenant cannot come to people who swear covenants with themselves. The process of healing begins as we forgive those who violated covenant with us *and* as we repent of the oaths we have sworn.

Additionally, we cannot replace one form of covenant with another. For instance, if you are a single parent, you cannot expect your twelve-year-old child to meet your emotional needs. He or she cannot be your confidant, your best friend and your refuge. By God's grace, though, you can maintain your covenant with that child even though your spouse broke covenant with you both.

Likewise, we must be careful not to confuse one covenant with another. Often, those with unbelieving spouses neglect their duties to that spouse in favour of fulfilling their covenant responsibilities to God. For example, they immerse themselves in church activities. Covenant with God does not release you from covenant with your spouse. The surest way for you to lead that spouse to the Lord is to convince him or her that God places high priority on marriage covenant.

Establishing New Covenants

How then can we establish new covenants if our old covenants have been broken? For the young woman whose husband deserted her and their three-year-old daughter, is there any prospect for new covenant with another man? What about the man whose wife has committed adultery for the third time after being forgiven for the previous two violations? Can he hope for another covenant that promises fidelity?

The focus of this book is not primarily divorce and remarriage—and I don't attempt a generic answer to the theological questions posed by the issue. Any decisions about divorce and remarriage should be brought to your local church to spiritual leaders who know the particulars of the Word of God and the particulars of your life. The counsel of trusted spiritual advisors who know you is *always* to be preferred over the counsel of a book.

But to help you formulate questions to ask yourself and your church leaders, let me offer a few thoughts about establishing new covenants.

1. Jesus is a redeemer, and the New Covenant points to our future more than to our past. God established a new covenant; in fact, He actually enacted several covenants with people before establishing the final covenant through Jesus Christ. When God forgives our past, we are freed from it. To hopelessly lock away the possibility of a new covenantal relationship because we violated or were violated in an old covenant seems out of step with the mercy and grace of God. However, to presume upon that grace and to divorce your spouse *for the express purpose* of marrying someone else is forbidden.

2. Human beings can have deceptive and hardened hearts. That is why God allows covenants of marriage to be dissolved. Divorce is never His first choice, but He knows that people do choose to close themselves off from His way. Though He hates divorce, He allows us to divorce a spouse for unfaithfulness, physical abuse or hardness of heart. Divorce itself isn't sin, but divorce is always caused by sin. Though God allows a way out of one covenant He does not necessarily intend to make a way into another covenant. Divorce and remarriage are not the same issue.

3. Without covenant with God through Jesus Christ,

we can't know the fullness of human covenants like marriage. Above all others we should commit to our covenant with the Lord. In the heartbreak that follows violated and broken marriage, humans tend to look for another human covenant to assuage the hurt. However, no human covenant promises the recovery and restoration that God's covenant extends to us. The myth of our culture is that we need to be married to be fulfilled and happy. In reality, many marriage covenants—especially second or third marriages—that are hastily made with wrong motives actually get in the way of God's covenant.

4. Most second or third marriages fail for many of the same reasons the original covenants were violated. Rarely is there a clear-cut culprit who single-handedly ruined the first marriage. Or perhaps more to the point, rarely can the victim of a violated marriage covenant enter a second marriage without bringing with him or her some seeds of destruction. Divorce is messy and infectious; it spawns spores of psycho-emotional damage that will inevitably be carried by both partners into any future covenants. Therefore, allow a significant amount of time for spiritual recovery after any divorce. You will never be healed by a second covenant; recovery from the first one must precede a second one.

5. All covenants are inconvenient to maintain. They require an unbelievable amount of sacrifice, selflessness, surrender and servanthood. Covenants are all about the others in the covenant, not about us. Marriage covenant is an offer made to secure our spouse, not to neatly arrange our own life. When one marriage covenant has been broken, the parties in that failed marriage get thrown back upon themselves; they become acutely aware of themselves as separate, distinct people—almost like adolescents going through the process of self-discovery.

Victims of abused or broken covenant are necessarily self-focused. As such, they are rarely in a place to offer to another person the kind of selfless and sacrificial covenant patterned by God. Having gone through the death of a covenant, they will usually be none too eager to die to themselves—a prerequisite for all true covenants. It is important, then, to ask what you really want—another relationship, or *covenant*.

A Simple Promise

I may be stirring the pot of painful memories in many of you—the pain and the emotion of looking at how things were in your family. The pain can come from acknowledging that your family experience was a far cry from what you understand God intended for you.

Maybe this discussion has rekindled painful memories, so that you relive some of the traumas you went through. All of this presents you with a bewildering array of emotions and inner turmoil. And that is to be expected. You have been hurt—that is hard. We have been broken and have had to live with anger, shame, guilt and confusion.

The Bible says Christ Jesus came into the world to rescue, to restore and to recover people who have done wrong or who have had wrong done to them. He came for people like you and me.

He has promised, as part of His covenant, never to leave us on our own, never to desert us when we have failed. He promises to lead us and guide us in His ways. His covenant will never be violated or betrayed. As we grow and develop within the secured sanctuary of God's relationship with us, we can know the abundant life He promises. Leave it to Him to lead you into whatever new relationships He has for you. That is the safest and surest way to live.

11

What Is Broken Can Be Fixed

When I talked to people in my church about the cry for covenant deep within our hearts, lights came on for husbands and wives, parents and children. Like Duane, people began to understand why they repeat in their own family the outrage and anger they experienced in their childhood. Cindy and other mums ambivalent about the prospect of having more (or any) children started to realise that families are the way they are not because of luck or fate, but because of how closely they follow the pattern of covenant.

I watched people like Josslyn and her husband pledge themselves to a pure and precious bonding with their own children completely void of any of the incestuous horror Josslyn knew as a young girl. Members of my congregation admitted that they really didn't know how to put a family together according to God's plan. They are like me and the pushchair assembly, only they are quicker to acknowledge the limitations of their 'know-how' when it comes to doing family God's way.

Barbara and Skip have learned to refuse the contractual offers of her parents, and have begun to move away from the deadly patterns of control and rejection she knew in her childhood.

Donny and Heather still have a way to go. Covenant does not answer every problem in a marriage, but at least the couple realise that their expectations of each other need a serious overhaul. They are working on creating a climate of forgiveness and affection.

I should not have been surprised by the responses I got from others. Living out a covenant relationship is entirely different from living out a contractual one. Contractual relationships anchor themselves to time and place. They give both parties the means to monitor the relationship and to sever it should either be found inadequate in carrying out his or her part of the agreement.

A contract is static, something we can point back to, like the document we signed in 1987 agreeing to purchase a home with a twenty-year mortgage. The terms are set out clearly, and the penalties are waiting if we fail to meet the terms. As any home owner knows, there is not much latitude for creative interpretation of the contract. We agreed to the terms, and if we fail to meet them, we forfeit the property. No exceptions.

Unfortunately, people can approach relationships in the same way. When a spouse, or in-laws, or teenage children do not meet the standards or terms they had in mind, they 'foreclose' on them.

How different that static arrangement is from the joy of covenant. That's what many of the people I shared these concepts with found out. They had been raised with contracts, and had unwittingly transferred them to their adult relationships and to their relationships with their children. But when they began to see the freedom of living in a covenant relationship, things they struggled with for years suddenly were no longer issues for them.

Not that everything was suddenly put right. Covenant

is not pixie dust we sprinkle on our family problems to make them disappear. But now these people had a completely different perspective on their struggles.

We all perform best in an encouraging and affirming environment devoid of ridicule and judgement. When we give those we live with an environment like that, we create conditions that invite them to change. This is especially true for our children. Remember, they have a strong innate desire to please their parents. Once we convince our children that we love them no matter what, they will want all the more to do the things that please us.

We cannot force change. Despite all you do in covenant, your spouse and children will have to choose for themselves how they want to live. But when you follow the four elements of true covenant, you maximise the likelihood of your family members joining you.

Rediscovering Covenant

When we find covenant, we have returned to basics—the basics of why we were made and how we were designed to relate to one another. The need for covenant is wired into our psyches, and when we find covenant, we find *home*.

But arriving at covenant is not like getting into a car, or putting on a new coat. It is something we already have, yet something we must work at. How can this be? Christianity is filled with paradoxes. For example, we are told that we are perfected in Christ, yet we battle with our imperfections. We are told that we are holy, a royal priesthood, but at the same time we are admonished to live worthy of our calling. We are told that we have freedom, yet we get bogged down in our sin and selfishness. We have all good things in Christ Jesus, yet we must learn to make them a reality in our lives.

Paul sums it up this way,

Not that I have already obtained all this, or have
already been made perfect, but I press on to take
hold of that for which Christ Jesus took hold of
me (Phil. 3:12).

We are all committed to a certain number of covenant
relationships, but we live them out imperfectly. It is so easy
to get side-tracked and attempt to realise the ideals of
covenant within the framework of contract.

How do we grow closer to the heart of covenant?
Obviously, we need to remind ourselves of the difference
between covenant family and dysfunctional family. Some of
you may have relationships that you now realise are built on
the shifting sand of contractual arrangements. Let's stop for
a moment to review our key relationships—the ones that
God intended to be covenantal.

Covenant with God

The first relationship we need to be concerned with is the
one we have with our heavenly Father. We have seen that
He unconditionally loves us; nothing we can do, no lack of
performance on our part, can ever erase that love. But do
we come to Him because our gratitude compels us? Or
because of what He can do for us? Are we using Him as a
kind of cosmic good-luck charm, thinking, *As long as I have
God on my side, nothing can go wrong for me. Or, God if you'll
just get me out of this mess I'll do anything you want me to.
Only don't let me down this time.*

God longs for a covenantal relationship with us—one
not based on a legalistic, you-do-that-and-as-a-trade-off-
I'll-do-this approach, but one based on grace. God wants

fellowship with us, heart to heart. He wants to be more than our master, more than our supplier, more than our protector, He wants to be our *friend*. Jesus told His disciples:

> I no longer call you servants, because a servant does not know his master's business. Instead, I have called you friends, for everything that I learned from my Father I have made known to you (John 15:15).

We are friends with God, in a relationship built on the desire to know each other intimately. Revitalising our covenant with Him is as easy as confessing our violations and asking Him to reveal more of Himself to us. His covenant always offers us hope.

Covenant in Marriage

The second relationship where each of us is to live up to the light of covenant is with our spouse. It is easy to think, *Well, when they pull their weight in these areas, I will get my act together in that area.* Over the years we adopt a do-unto-them-as-they-have-done-unto-me attitude, excusing our shortcomings by dwelling on those of our spouse. Such mental gymnastics might well help us to avoid facing our own problems, but they certainly will not build the type of marriage we dreamed of.

And, really, the relationship between husband and wife is the basic building block of any family. Sometimes I counsel a person with a poor relationship with their spouse who thinks they can overcome the ill-effects on their children by compensating them in other ways. There is no gift that can make up for a poor relationship between Mum and Dad.

A marriage that is dead at the heart is like a tree that is dead at the root—eventually it will strangle the life and joy out of everything that depends on it. The good news is, even dead marriages can be resurrected in God's Kingdom.

In most cases it will not be a sudden, Lazarus-type of resurrection. Restoration is often slow and painful because it involves transformation. Your thinking has begun to change. You long for covenant, but you will still reap a residue of past dealings and hurts. Don't become impatient with your spouse, with yourself or with the process. Like Lazarus, we have to be unbound from our grave clothes.

Habits, patterns of speech, reactions to each other, even the way you spend your time and money—these are some of the burial garments that will have to be unwrapped from your marriage. The beauty of covenant is that you now have new patterns to follow.

You can concentrate on promoting and celebrating your spouse's uniqueness. Compliment your spouse on those qualities. Dwell on them when you are apart, and let the Holy Spirit restore and enlarge your desire for your spouse. Disciplining your thoughts to be positive towards your covenant partner can eventually lead to an anticipation for them as strong as that felt by someone newly in love.

Also, focus on developing a new history with your partner. Replace past arguments and mistakes with creative, pleasant times together. Start dating again. Send cards. Surprise your spouse with pleasures—not your definition of pleasures, but his or hers. A new history together will revitalise the dormant power of covenant to rain blessings on you both.

Another covenant element you can utilise is making vows. Some couples in our church have renewed their wedding vows by re-enacting the ceremony or by inviting friends to witness anew their pledges to one another. This activity alone will not salvage a marriage, but the more we promise ourselves to our partner, the more we unlock the power of covenant. There's power in speaking aloud the decisions of the heart. Confession is powerful, especially when it follows the pattern of covenant. Start making little but meaningful promises, then keep them. It will turn your spouse's head—and eventually, his or her heart.

Covenant with Our Children

Third, we may be facing the reality that we have used our children for our own ends. We have expected them to live up to *our* expectations for them, and rewarded them with our attention and approval only when they do so. Instead of living out a two-way relationship with them, we've been content to be the authority figure, the person who yells 'jump', after which they ask 'how high?' Now we can see that there is more to living out covenant with our children than that. We have the responsibility to know who they are and to help them develop into all that they can be. What a challenge! We switch from the controller to the cheer-leader—and that's not easy for some parents.

That is why this last chapter is devoted mostly to the question, *How can I turn around the damage I have already done to my children, and begin living out true family covenant with them?*

Wanting to be Better Parents

The first time I grasped the notion of family covenant, I was immediately struck by profound personal implications—about why I am the way I am, but more importantly, about what I can do for my children. Covenant tells us much about how we were parented and about how we can parent.

I must admit I am most keen on the ideas covenant offers for being the kind of father I always dreamed of being. No matter how dysfunctional our upbringing may have been, we entertain the hope that we can do better or more for our children than our parents did for us. If nothing else, we promise ourselves we will be a different kind of parent; we will handle things differently; we will treat our children the way we wish we had been treated. But not all of what our parents did was wrong, so we will also follow patterns of parenting we learned from them. Some of these patterns may be dysfunctional, but some make sense. Not everything our parents did was abusive.

Practically speaking, we want to build on our parents' foundation—discarding and avoiding some of how they raised us, but adopting and copying other aspects of their parenting. What motivates us to pick and choose is our sincere desire to be great parents to our children. Learning about covenant and its power is an important step towards being better parents to our children and better partners for our spouses. Covenant empowers families like Collin's remote-controlled car. But the purpose of that power is to move the family along. Where should I take my family? What should I do to unlock the incredible dynamic of family covenant in order to bless my children?

It's Never Too Late

To gain perspective on family covenant and our job as parents, let's look at our covenant with God through Jesus Christ. As we do, remember that it is never too late to turn things around in your family.

The New Covenant points us to the future with

promises of what we can do and become because of God's power working in us. The old covenant of the law kept us looking backwards at the wrong things we had done. Our past shaped our future. But under the New Covenant, God's forgiveness eliminates the power of our past. Acknowledging the wrong we have done in our children's lives is, therefore, the first step in changing the way we parent them.

Sure we have 'missed it' as parents. We have said foolish things; we have been selfish with our time and energy; we have walked away from chances to be with the children because we were too intent on our own agenda. It shouldn't be a surprise that we have done an imperfect job.

I do not want to skip glibly over our failure as parents as though those failures are no big deal. But we do not help our children by staying stuck there. God forgives us. And so will our children. They do not have much of an idea about *good parenting*, all they know is they want to be close to us. If we will humble ourselves and ask them to forgive us for our lost temper, our busyness, our inconsistency, they will welcome us into their arms. Sin destroys relationship. Our sins separate us from God and our sins as parents separate us from our children. But under family covenant we can be forgiven if we acknowledge our failures to God *and* to our children. It may take a while for some children to relent, but if they continue to see us earnestly longing to renew lost relationship, they will eventually come around.

Removing Guilt

The New Covenant offers an answer to our guilt. But as long as we still think in terms of the old covenant, we won't come clean and admit our failures. Instead, we try to ignore our faults, and end up with vague feelings of guilt rather than specific points of failure that can be confessed and forgiven.

Admitting your shortcomings as a parent renews your family covenant with your children. Even if there are too many failures to count, at least get started with the most recent episodes. Start confessing your failures as they occur, and you will be amazed at how your family will heal. And it will establish a pattern of living for children to follow.

As a thirteen-year-old I learned in science that matter doesn't disappear; it just changes form. I thought that was amazing. I always thought that if you burn something up, it was gone except for the ashes. Science taught me instead that it has turned into other kinds of matter and energy.

The same is true of guilt. You can't get rid of it on your own. The human soul was not designed to do that. Guilt is meant to be absorbed by God. The covenant God established with us welcomes us into His family where all of our wrong and all of our guilt can be absorbed (forgiven) if we will acknowledge it. He takes it all and keeps it away from us. That is also what family does. When I willingly acknowledge that I did wrong, my family can absorb that guilt, and it doesn't have to affect how they feel about me. My wrong, if truly repented of, is not some kind of baggage that I hang in my heart from that point on in my life.

Shame and guilt are pervasive in our culture. But family has the awesome power to prevent shame and guilt from destroying children—by distinguishing between family members and the things those members do. The old adage 'hate the sin, not the sinner', is exactly what family is called to do for its members.

Unconditional love means that under no circumstances and for no reason will a child feel unloved. In true family, children do not feel that their relationships with Mum and Dad depend on doing everything right. Gaining, then retaining, parents' favour and affection is not based on the rightness or wrongness of what a child does or thinks. Relationships rest on covenant. Covenant establishes and maintains relationships far more powerfully than individuals in a family can by their own personalities or performance.

For children who sense they are loved even when their behaviour is not, right and wrong become moral issues rather than emotional issues. Unconditional love provides a child with the first and most important step in moral development—the ability to distinguish between self and sin: 'I am loved by my parents. I know that. What I just did to hurt my little sister is not loved by them. Therefore, I am not what I just did.'

When parents label a child as *bad*—because of the child's unacceptable behaviour—they blur the border between the child's self and the child's sin. If children don't learn to differentiate between what they do and who they are, they can grow up with a poor self-image that must be constantly propped up by perfectionism. Only when children feel loved regardless of what they do will they develop healthy self-esteem. Unconditional love in family gives children emotional and psychological security for a lifetime, removing questions about personal identity. Family lays the foundation for most of their conceptions about themselves.

Guilt and love cannot coexist. The bigger one is, the smaller the other becomes. So, the more we love our children, the less they will feel guilty. Also, the more we rid ourselves of our guilt over our failures as parents, the more we will be able to freely love our family.

Feelings of Inadequacy

Besides struggling with guilt, we parents can struggle with feelings of inadequacy. We don't feel we have what it takes to be great parents. Parenting can seem like a talent or a gift that only a few people have. The rest of us have to make do with meagre attempts. We disqualify ourselves because of our past or because of our current ignorance. We read book after book on parenting, yet it all seems so complicated. But the New Covenant is more about love than it is about knowledge. And God's love for our children will motivate us to be the best possible parents.

I do not want to imply that we can successfully parent our children by following any pattern we might devise on our own—just as long as we love them. As we have learned, God has a specific pattern for family. We parents are given detailed instructions for how to raise our children. Although we have to apply ourselves and learn somethings, we will never feel that we know enough to be good parents—love must carry the day.

There is another reason for our feelings of inadequacy as parents. It goes beyond the importance of loving our children, to the root of our life in God. Simply put, we need God. We need His example as a parent, His grace, His support and His instruction. Our inadequacy points us to His adequacy. Our incompleteness and brokenness enable us to fully open up to His wholeness. He has what we need, and our need gives Him an opportunity to parent us.

This is not some religious cliché. It is central to the way the New Covenant operates. Our confidence is not in ourselves or in our own abilities, but in Jesus Christ. That is why Paul gladly boasts about his weaknesses, for when we are weak, then we are strong in the power of Christ (2 Cor. 12:9–10). His grace is there for us as parents. If we will ask

Him, He will teach us how to parent. He reveals His way not to the wise, but to simple people of faith; if we come to Him and learn from him, we will find restful answers for the awesome task of parenting. That is part of His family covenant with us. How wonderful that His covenant helps us to keep our covenant with our children!

Besides admitting our failures, another step to revitalising covenant relationship with children is to acknowledge our constant need for the Lord. This means taking time to ask Him how to respond to challenges, and it means studying what God tells us in His Word about parenting.

I am amazed at the number of parents who unknowingly, or knowingly, disregard straightforward direction in the Bible on child rearing. Being inadequate to the task of parenting is one thing. Being inattentive to the advice of God on the subject is another. Though we do not have the time to detail all those biblical commands in this book, I encourage you to study them on your own and with the help of your church leaders. How instructive is God's Word for those of us who want to become better parents? Let's see.

Training Kids

Established covenant produces a secure environment in which children can grow and experience life. Family covenant is like an old shoe that has become familiar with the imprint of a foot. Old shoes are comfortable. In the same way, children raised in covenant family will long for the comfortable 'feel' of that family, even when they are grown.

Hence, family life establishes what is normal and what should be expected by the child in adulthood. Family has incredible power to secure children for the rest of their lives. There is a scriptural statement acknowledging family as a culture that indelibly imprints its, customs and patterns on children:

> Train up a child in the way he should go, and when he is old he will not turn from it (Prov. 22:6).

Family marks children for the rest of their lives. That's true whether it is for good or evil. In other words, *family is habit forming*. Throughout life, children find themselves drawn to the kind of environment they experienced when they were younger.

When Scripture speaks of training-up children in the way they should go, it talks about two specific things. First, training a child literally means to *narrow* a child. It doesn't mean whittling them down or cutting them down to size: 'This kid is too big for his britches; I'll teach him.' Many parents foolishly think discipline is meant to bring a child down a notch. That is not God's intent for discipline. Godly discipline means narrowing the boundaries in your daughter's and son's lives so they are not left free to wander off on their own.

The *narrowing* might be as simple as telling our children what kind of things 'we don't do in our family'. Recently, I spent some time with a pastor-couple who adopted a little boy from Romania. As an orphan, this boy learned how to live in cut-throat circumstances. He learned to swear and to make obscene gestures when he was angry. Almost one year after this boy came to live with my friends, they still had to remind him, 'We don't do that in our family.' They persistently *reinforce* appropriate limits for him. A family is like a culture, and a child is *initiated* into the ways, habits, customs, beliefs and the functioning of that culture.

The second meaning of *training* a child is *initiating* or *introducing*. To introduce them to the world, we say things to our children like, 'This is how we use our spoon; right side up. It works better that way.' Family initiates and introduces children to the ways of the world—how things are done, how things are expressed, how life is lived.

By watching family, a child can tell, 'Oh, this is how the world works.' For example, we parents can introduce our children to sharing, forgiving or serving. As we left home for a work party at our church, my youngest, Evan, was unhappy that he couldn't stay and play with the neighbourhood kids. When he asked why he had to help at church, I told him serving is always better than getting our own way. He was not convinced.

Later in the day, when I found him pulling weeds from the church lawn with a buddy, I asked him if he was having fun.

'Yeah,' he said.

'You see,' I told him, 'serving is lots of fun.' Introduction *and* follow-through in our children's lives become part of their unconscious world views that serve them later in life.

Don't Exasperate Your Kids

Are parents of undisciplined children any more exasperated than those children? No. Parental exasperation results mostly from parental sins or mistakes—not doing family God's way. Children are more the product of parental choices than of their own wilful choices. Our own blindness or ignorance creates frustration for ourselves and for our children. That is why Paul warns, 'Fathers do not exasperate your children, that they may not lose heart' (Col. 3:21 NASB). To *exasperate* means to aggravate to the point of anger, frustration or futility. An exasperated child feels there is no point in trying any longer. Parents unintentionally drive their children to frustration in ways beyond things we say or do. Let me give you some examples of exasperating children:

1. **Constantly nagging them.** Always finding something wrong with their hair, their friends, their bedroom.

2. **Making them feel their efforts are never good enough.** Focusing not on the decent grades they got, but on the better grades they could get; the more effort they could put out in sports; other ways they could style their hair to make it more flattering.

3. **Living vicariously through them.** Selfishly trying to use their lives to satisfy an emptiness in our own, like turning an eight-year-old into a best friend, or pushing a skating career to unreasonable limits.

4. **Relying on a legalistic atmosphere.** Maintaining a home filled with rules and prohibitions rather than with love and encouragement; putting more emphasis on threats, intimidations and restrictions than on promises, welcomes and possibilities.

The Bible provides us with excellent balance. We cannot be good parents without *training* our children, but neither can we fulfil our covenant responsibility to them by being so rigid that we *discourage* them.

Adopting a Hopeful Posture

Nothing is more spiritual than raising and nurturing our children in the family of God. And our covenant with God contains provisions that are designed to help us with all the particulars of our lives. But what if we have not kept our part of the covenant with our children? We do not want to do any more damage to them than we already have. What can we do? How can we be the parents our children need? An answer is found in Paul's exhortation to the Ephesians, when he talks about the *spiritual* nature of life's conflicts:

> Stand firm then, with the belt of truth buckled around your waist, with the breastplate of righteousness in place, and with your feet fitted with the readiness that comes from the gospel of peace. In addition to all this, take up the shield of faith, with which you can extinguish all the flaming arrows of the evil one. Take the helmet of salvation and the sword of the Spirit, which is the word of God. And pray in the Spirit on all occasions with all kinds of prayers and requests. With this in mind, be alert and always keep on praying for all the saints (Eph. 6:14–18).

I find here nine guidelines that can help us become more effective parents within the covenant of family. Effective parents are characterised by:

1. **Truth.** Sort things out carefully. Some things you have done are wrong, but not everything. Identify points of God's grace and strength. The truth is you do not have to do it all on your own. God is there.

2. **Righteousness.** Don't slip into the trap of self-condemnation or self-justification. God establishes our righteousness through forgiveness, not through our perfection. Remember the difference between being righteous and being right. Righteousness is mostly an issue of being obedient to what He says to us.

3. **Repentance.** Learning new ways to think and act as a parent. Be open to asking for forgiveness for old ways.

The good news begins with repentance, which means to reconsider, to come to different conclusions. 'What must I change in how I live?' The more you ask that, the more God will teach you.

4. **Faith.** Trust God and His Word. Like all of life, parenting is a walk of faith. The world tells us one way to raise our children; God tells us another. Choosing His way takes faith.

5. **Salvation.** God rescues and delivers us even when we do not deserve it. He helps us because of His grace, not because of our efforts or our ability to do everything right. God will also protect and preserve our children from the inadequacies of our parenting.

6. **The Word of God.** Learn and follow what the Bible says about parenting. The more we ingest God's Word, the more it writes itself over the wrong words previously written there. The Bible renews our thinking in ways that we cannot explain. The Bible is the Word of God's covenant within us.

7. **Prayer and Petition.** Never underestimate prayer. Much of what can harm our children is beyond our ability to control. Remembering that God loves our children more than we do makes it easier to trust them to him. Prayer provides for and protects our family.

8. **Alertness.** Look for little concerns before they become big concerns. Not only watch out for children's physical safety, but also pay attention to subtle signals in their behaviour, conversations and attitudes. Vigilant parents rescue their children from dangerous emotions and attitudes before those things gain a toehold in their lives.

9. **Perseverance.** Be consistent in your expectations, responses and behaviour. Persevere in attempts to establish

covenant with your children—it will eventually rescue them.

A Final Word on Covenant

Because covenant is not static, none of us can claim to have perfected it, to have 'arrived'. But neither should we despair if we have not lived out family covenant perfectly in our past. All is not lost.

The power of family is the power of covenant. Our violations of family covenant have had dire consequences for us, our spouses and our children. The violations of covenant committed by our parents have profoundly affected us all. Our dysfunctional upbringing and our imperfect parenting obscure God's plan for family to bless us all the days of our lives.

Things have not turned out this way by accident or fate. We know the cause of the dysfunction and damage. Our families are broken, and we are broken, because God's pattern of covenant has been violated. And knowing the cause is the most critical step in discovering the cure.

We have seen throughout this book that people's lives can be ruined by the very thing that promises to restore them: the power of family, the power of covenant. You can restore the power of covenant to the beneficial force it was meant by God to be. And by carefully attending to the four elements of true covenant—exchanging names, rehearsing history, making promises and accepting consequences—you can shape a bright future for your spouse and for your children.

You don't have to stay stuck with the consequences of your past. With God's help you can sow fresh seeds that will produce bountiful crops in your family. As you do so, continually remind yourself of the fulfilment of living out

God's loving design for your life—covenant with God, with your spouse and with your children. Within those boundaries you will find all that your heart cries for.

The power of family is covenant. And when we unlock that power, we have found *home*.

Photograph by Mary Fox Photography 1994

Pictured from left:
The Browns—Hilary, Lorrel, Pamela, Daniel, Evan and Collin.

About the Author

In each generation, God singles out a handful of men and women to speak truth in a fresh way to their contemporaries. Daniel A. Brown is one of those refreshing new voices of truth for our generation.

Ever since his days as a student at UCLA, Daniel's life has been marked by radical obedience to his Lord—an utter willingness to follow the slightest urging of the King. While a university student, his comfortable faith was challenged by the Jesus of his childhood, who wanted to become the Lord of his life.

From 1970 to 1977, Daniel led numerous small group Bible studies for UCLA students, while he completed an MA in literature. One of these studies grew to a weekly fellowship of nearly 200 participants.

After serving as a college instructor at a junior college, he joined the faculty of LIFE Bible College in Los Angeles, eventually moving into the position of director of college relations.

Daniel began attending The Church On The Way in Van Nuys, Califomia, and in 1979, he joined the pastoral staff to direct the college-career ministry. This group rapidly grew to one of the largest of its kind in California. In 1984, Daniel and his wife, Pamela, led a small company of collegians and young singles from Van Nuys to Aptos to pioneer a new church—The Coastlands.

Through Daniel's teaching and nurture at The Coastlands, leaders have been developed who have gone on to establish twenty-five new churches here and abroad.

Nurturing is the word most often used by Daniel's colleagues to describe his life and ministry. His teaching and thinking focus on developing people to their fullest potential, and releasing them to their own significant ministry. In his characteristic servant-leader demeanour, he'll tell you his congregation of nearly 1000 is designed to run itself. 'When I'm not there,' Daniel says, 'the church can run without me.'

Another comment he often makes is 'preaching should be fun.' His teaching style is practical, confrontational and challenging, often employing humour and drama. Although he has a doctorate from UCLA, Daniel always stresses the simple truths, referring repeatedly to 'the simplicity and purity of devotion to Christ' (2 Cor. 11:3).

Daniel's life passions include church planting, church growth and innovative approaches to ministry. He loves jogging, fishing and golf. But most of all, he loves Pamela, his wife of twenty years, and their four children, Hilary, 18, Collin, 15, Lorrel, 12, and Evan, 9.

When Love is Not Enough

Stephen Arterburn and Jim Burns

An indispensable tool for parents.

- To help parents prevent crisis situations
- To encourage parents whose children are already in crisis

'It's a tough world out there. Tougher still for today's youth. Drug addiction, teenage pregnancy, dropping out of school, suicide, peer pressure—all of these weigh heavily on the minds of our young people. There are, however, several options to reduce the negative risk factors for our lives and our children.'

'There is hope for those of us who are not perfect. Kids are resilient. They can take a lot. There are some awfully big problems in our world, but there are also some pretty wonderful families who have struggled and are making it one step at a time.'

Stephen Arterburn and Jim Burns

Stephen Arterburn and Jim Burns work every day with families in crisis. They believe that parents do not have to stand helplessly by and watch their children wander down paths of destruction. This indispensable handbook for parents offers understanding and practical tools to deal with crisis situations. Guidelines help any family prevent problems before they develop.

Catalogue Number YB 9575 £4.25

Guiding Your Family in a Misguided World

Dr Anthony Evans

- It used to be that parents could turn on the television set with confidence, knowing their children could watch decent programmes that promoted positive family values. Not any more.

- It used to be that parents could safely allow their children to play all day in the street, in the local neighbourhood, knowing the neighbours cared and ordinary people would keep an eye on the children and reinforce decent behaviour. Not any more.

- It used to be that schools were safe sanctuaries of education and learning that proved to be a positive basis in fostering a love for God and concern for the nation. Not any more.

In our increasingly misguided world, pastor and father Dr Anthony Evans shows parents how to lead their families in healthy, Christ-centred living.

The author starts by pinpointing some of the dangers facing the home today. He continues by showing how the family can still be a place of refuge, of safety and stability in the confusion that reigns. Finally, he explains how to pass on our own Christian values and faith to the next generation, so that the youth of today are prepared and able to stand on their own tomorrow.

Catalogue Number YB 9552   £3.99

Honouring Marriage

John & Liz Wilthew

Honouring Marriage is a practical workbook for those who are married, whether newly-weds or not-so-newly-weds. You will find many issues to challenge and inspire you to honour your marriage. The authors show us from a biblical base how to overcome real barriers to an openness and freedom which demonstrates God's love in marriage. With many practical exercises and assignments this could be used by individual couples or together in a group setting as part of a study course.

Catalogue Number YB 9188   £2.99

Parenting Isn't for Cowards

Dr James Dobson

Here is a celebration of parenthood at a time when parents are suffering a crisis of confidence as they cope with children of different temperaments, struggle with the pressures of an immoral society and furthermore, get blamed whenever anything goes wrong with one of their offspring. 'I just can't cope,' was a common reply in a survey Dr Dobson conducted among 35,000 parents. He affirms that parenthood can be a joyful experience, and gives practical, specific advice to parents 'trying to raise their children in a shock-wave world'.

Catalogue Number YB 9148   £2.95

The Two Sides of Love

Gary Smalley and John Trent

- Are you tired of coming close to intimacy but never quite reaching it?

- Does your spouse possess some traits that you loved during courtship but that drive you crazy now?

- Are you frustrated by an inability to motivate your child except through physical discipline?

- Do you struggle to be firm and decisive—and sometimes say no—even when that's what you and your loved ones need?

- Or do you struggle to show love and affection, to encourage as well as criticise?

We all long for stronger, closer, more affectionate relationships. The key to developing them is to balance love's hard and soft sides every day. We need the hardness to discipline and protect. But we also need the softness to sympathise and encourage. And we need to understand the personalities of those closest to us so we can know which side of love they need at a given time.

In *The Two Sides of Love*, Gary Smalley and Dr John Trent explore the two halves of wholehearted love and offer practical counsel for getting and keeping relationships in a healthy, Christlike balance.

Catalogue Number YB 9233   £3.25